MACMILLAN MODERN NOVELISTS

General Editor: Norman Page

MODERN NOVELISTS

MACMILLAN MODERN NOVELISTS
JOHN FOWLES

James Acheson

First published 1998 by
MACMILLAN PRESS LTD
Houndmills, Basingstoke, Hampshire RG21 6XS
and London
Companies and representatives throughout the world

ISBN 0-333-51669-9 hardcover
ISBN 0-333-51670-2 paperback

A catalogue record for this book is available from the British Library.

This book is printed on paper suitable for recycling and
made from fully managed and sustained forest sources.

10 9   8   7   6 5   4   3   2   1
07 06 05 04 03 02 01 00 99 98

Editing and origination by
Aardvark Editorial, Mendham, Suffolk

Printed in Hong Kong

 Published in the United States of America 1998 by
ST. MARTIN'S PRESS, INC.,
Scholarly and Reference Division,
175 Fifth Avenue, New York, N.Y. 10010

ISBN 0-312-21387-5

For Carole – with all my love

Contents

General Editor's Preface

The death of the novel has often been announced, and part of the secret of its obstinate vitality must be its capacity for growth, adaptation, self-renewal and self-transformation; like some vigorous organism in a speeded-up Darwinian ecosystem, it adapts itself quickly to a changing world. War and revolution, economic crisis and social change, radically new ideologies such as Marxism and Freudianism, have made this century unprecedented in human history in the speed and extent of change, but the novel has shown an extraordinary capacity to find new forms and techniques and to accommodate new ideas and conceptions of human nature and human experience, and even to take up new positions on the nature of fiction itself.

In the generations immediately preceding and following 1914, the novel underwent a radical redefinition of its nature and possibilities. The present series of monographs is devoted to the novelists who created the modern novel and to those who, in their turn, either continued and extended, or reacted against and rejected, the traditions established during that period of intense exploration and experiment. It includes a number of those who lived and wrote in the nineteenth century but whose innovative contribution to the art of fiction makes it impossible to ignore them in any account of the origins of the modern novel; it also includes the so-called 'modernists' and those who in the mid- and late twentieth century have emerged as outstanding practitioners of this genre. The scope is, inevitably, international; not only, in the migratory and exile-haunted world of our century, do writers refuse to heed national frontiers – 'English' literature lays claim to Conrad the Pole, Henry James the American and Joyce the Irishman – but geniuses such as Flaubert, Dostoevsky and Kafka have had an influence on the fiction of many nations.

Each volume in the series is intended to provide an introduction to the fiction of the writer concerned, both for those approaching him or her for the first time and for those who are already familiar with some parts of the achievement in question and now wish to place it in the context of the total *œuvre*. Although essential information relating to the writer's life and times is given, usually in an opening chapter, the approach is primarily critical and the emphasis is not upon 'background' or generalisations but open, close examination of important texts. Where an author is notably prolific, major texts have been made to convey, more summarily, a sense of the nature and quality of the author's work as a whole. Those who want to read further will find suggestions in the select bibliography included in each volume.

Many novelists are, of course, not only novelists but also poets, essayists, biographers, dramatists, travel writers and so forth; many have practised shorter forms of fiction; and many have written letters or kept diaries that constitute a significant part of their literary output. A brief study cannot hope to deal with all these in detail, but where the shorter fiction, and the non-fictional writings, public and private, have an important relationship to the novels, some space has been devoted to them.

NORMAN PAGE

Preface

John Fowles is at the same time a best-selling novelist and one who attracts the attention of undergraduate students, thesis writers and professional academics. To the casual reader, he is a novelist who writes so well, who creates such an aura of suspense and intrigue, that it is difficult to put his books down. To the scholar, Fowles is a writer whose interest in existentialism manifests itself in his early novels, *The Collector* (1963), *The Magus* (1965) and *The French Lieutenant's Woman* (1969), but wanes from *The Ebony Tower* (1974) through to *Daniel Martin* (1977) and *A Maggot* (1985). Fowles is particularly interested in the achievement of existential authenticity – the process by which the individual exchanges his conventional ideas and attitudes for ones that are consistent with the person he or she really is. In each of his early novels, Fowles presents us with characters who are living conventional lives and mouthing conventional opinions, then shows us how these characters either succeed or fail at gaining greater self-knowledge in response to the situation in which he places them. What follows is an examination of his early enthusiasm for existentialism, and of how his approach to fiction writing changed from the mid-1970s onwards.

I should like to thank my colleagues, William Walker and Peter Tremewan, for reading parts of this study and making many helpful suggestions. Another colleague, Gordon Spence, was very helpful with Chapter 7, on *A Maggot*. I also wish to thank the University of Canterbury for granting me the study leave and travel funding that enabled me to complete it.

Finally, I would like to thank my wife Carole, to whom this book is dedicated, for her patience, good humour and consistently stimulating conversation on all matters related to English literature.

JAMES ACHESON
Christchurch, New Zealand

x

Acknowledgements

The author and publishers wish to thank Mr John Fowles and his agents, Sheil Land Associates Ltd, for permission to reprint extracts from *The Collector* (copyright c.1963); rpt London: Triad/Panther, 1976), *The Magus* (copyright c.1965; rev. edn 1977; London: Triad/ Panther, 1978), *The French Lieutenant's Woman* (copyright c.1969; rpt London: Panther, 1972), *The Ebony Tower* (copyright c.1974; rpt London: Pan, 1986), *Daniel Martin* (copyright c.1977; rpt London: Triad/Grafton, 1986), and *A Maggot* (copyright c.1985; rpt London: Pan, 1986).

1

Introduction

John Fowles has the distinction of being both a best-selling novelist and one whose work has earned the respect of academic critics. Why his novels are best-sellers is clear enough. Like Daniel Defoe, a writer he greatly admires, Fowles has tremendous narrative drive, the ability to compel his readers' attention from the beginning of his novels through to the end.[1] Fowles so beguiles us with uncertainty in his fiction, so tantalises us with a variety of possible outcomes, that we read his novels and short stories eagerly to find out what happens in the end. Will Frederick Clegg, the twisted clerk in *The Collector* (1963), rape Miranda, the attractive young woman he has taken captive? Will he be responsible in some way for her death? Alternatively, will he take pity on her and let her go? Will Nicholas Urfe, the main character of *The Magus* (1965), make his way safely through the 'godgame' that the mysterious Maurice Conchis has chosen to play with him? How will this all-important game affect the rest of his life? Will Charles Smithson, the main character of *The French Lieutenant's Woman* (1969), leave his fiancée, Ernestina Freeman, for Sarah Woodruff, a woman whose haunting eyes draw him to her, just as the sirens' songs lured sailors to shipwreck? Or will he marry Ernestina and spend the rest of his life living as a conventional Victorian gentleman, bitterly regretting having made a colossal mistake? Such questions as these arise not only in *The Collector*, *The Magus* and *The French Lieutenant's Woman*, but in all of Fowles's novels, and the reader's curiosity about the answers does not always stop short of prurience.

For it must be acknowledged that another reason Fowles's novels are best sellers is that sex figures prominently in all of them. *The Collector* tells of a young man's kidnapping of a girl for what he imagines are romantic, but are in fact perverted sexual purposes. Similarly, *The Magus* concerns a young man who initially finds the callous, unloving

1

seduction of a series of women more satisfactory than having long-term serious relationships; while _Daniel Martin_ (1977) tells of a middle-aged man who drifts from one sexually charged, short-term affair to another before finally deciding to marry a woman he has known since university. Similarly, Fowles's first historical novel, _The French Lieutenant's Woman_, reveals that the sexual puritanism of the Victorians was no more than a hypocritical sham. Though Victorian gentlemen often wrote or spoke of the importance of observing a strict sexual rectitude, the novel makes it clear that prostitution was much more widespread in the nineteenth century than in our own, and that many of the prostitutes' clients were the moralistic gentlemen in question. Finally, _A Maggot_ (1985), Fowles's most recent novel, shows that prostitution played an important part in the early eighteenth century as well, though in a far less hypocritical climate. One of _A Maggot_'s main characters, Rebecca Lee, is a London prostitute who is taken on an extraordinary journey by a mysterious Mr Bartholomew, in the course of which he obliges her to copulate with his manservant while he observes them. Voyeurism, prostitution, kidnapping for sexual purposes – all this and more is to be found in Fowles's novels, though he treats these subjects with a notable seriousness of purpose.[2]

Fowles includes the erotic in his novels because, as he has said, 'I teach better if I seduce'.[3] What he seeks to teach us is the importance of striving to understand ourselves better, and of founding relationships on friendship and trust rather than just on sexual attraction. The right kind of relationships, he emphasises in his fiction, can be highly educational, and especially so for the male of the species, since men are more likely than women to need help coming to terms with their sexuality. For Fowles, masculinity is an 'appalling crust' that filters everything men hear and see.[4] This 'crust' is especially rigid, Fowles told Sarah Benton in a 1983 interview, in those who went through public school and military service. 'The crude things in men', he commented, 'should be educated out of them and jettisoned.'[5] Women are a civilising influence on men, Fowles went on to say, and although men have dominated them for generations, there have been occasional periods of history in which society has been dominated by women, times that have been highly fruitful and productive.

In _The Aristos_, a collection of aphorisms he began as an undergraduate, Fowles comments that

Adam is stasis, or conservatism; Eve is kinesis, or progress. Adam societies are ones in which the man and the father, male gods, exact strict obedience to established institutions and norms of behaviour, as during a majority of the periods of history in our era. The Victorian is a typical such period. Eve societies are those in which the woman and the mother, female gods, encourage innovation and experiment, and fresh definitions, aims, modes of feeling. The Renaissance and our own are typical such ages.[6]

If male-dominated periods are characterised by unimaginative conservatism, it is clear that the impact on such a period of a single, extraordinary woman must be great. Sarah Woodruff plays the role of such a woman in *The French Lieutenant's Woman*, broadening the mind of Charles Smithson, a conventional Victorian gentleman, and finding her way into the Eve-dominated society of the Rossettis. Her counterpart in *A Maggot*, Rebecca Lee, though at first a common prostitute, ultimately brings to the Adam society of the early eighteenth century the mystery and wonder of an extraordinary vision. Rebecca may not have a great influence on her own generation, but Fowles tells us that Ann Lee, her putative daughter, became one of the founders of the Shakers, a religious group that was formed in the north of England and set up a Utopian, Eve-dominated community in the United States.

Whether in novels set in previous centuries or in our own, Fowles is intrigued by the influence women have over men. 'Women', he says in *The Aristos*, 'know more about human nature, more about mystery, and more about keeping passion alive [than men do]' (90). Women have the power to inspire men in a variety of ways. For Fowles it is entirely appropriate that the classical Muses, the sources of varying kinds of imaginative inspiration, should have been female. In a short novel entitled *Mantissa* (1982) – a novel too minor to warrant a chapter's discussion in the present study – Erato, a Muse, makes herself known to the writer Miles Green in a variety of forms.[7] Unfortunately for Fowles, none of Erato's guises is 'attractive to a feminist, from the punk-like harridan who abuses the man in slabs of hackneyed reproach', as Sarah Benton observes, 'to the nymphette who finds an unexpected pleasure in being raped by a satyr'.[8] Fowles may be fascinated by women, and highly sympathetic to the fact that they must take second place in a male-dominated world, but this does not mean that he is always politically correct.

Indeed, in an interview with Katherine Tarbox in 1988, Fowles was at pains to stress that he had great sympathy not for 'feminism in the modern sense, but for a female principle in life. It doesn't always tie in with modern feminism. My wife would deny point blank that I'm a proper feminist. But I do, more for obscure personal reasons, hate the macho viewpoint.'[9] His female characters are often mentors – Alison in *The Magus*, Sarah in *The French Lieutenant's Woman*, and Jane in *Daniel Martin*, to name three examples – and it is as the result of their counsel that the leading male character in each novel becomes a better human being.

Nevertheless, Fowles believes that it is not altogether the women who influence his male characters for good. In the interview with Katherine Tarbox he speaks of his interest in Jung's theory of the anima – in brief, the theory that in every man there is a feminine component, just as in every woman there is a masculine component, the animus.[10] Getting in touch with the anima is very important for a man, Fowles believes, and especially important for sensitive, intelligent men, the ones who stand to gain most by shattering the 'crust' of masculinity and becoming aware of the unencumbered self that lies within them.

Fowles's interest in the importance of helping men to come to a clearer understanding of themselves arose from his schooling and experience of being in the Marines. Born in 1926, he was sent to Bedford School, and in due course became a member of the first eleven at cricket, as well as head boy, with the power to flog fellow students at will. Under him, he told Mark Amory in 1974, was a 'police force of sixty... prefects and sub-prefects. You held court every morning and flogged the guilty.' Asked if he had any doubts about his role at the time, Fowles replied, 'I don't think so. I mustn't pretend. Lots of guilt ever since.'[11] But the guilt did not begin until years later. When he joined the Marines during the Second World War, he put in for officer training without much enthusiasm, since 'Looking forward to having control of thirty marines was nothing when you had had control of eight hundred little boys, whom you could court-martial at a moment's whim. It was like offering Attila the Hun the mayoralty of a small English town.'[12] Fowles was made an officer, and was thinking of remaining in the military after the war, when

Isaac Foot, who was Lord Mayor of Plymouth, came to the mess and I was the young lieutenant deputed to look after him. I happened to put it to him and he thought it was preposterous that anyone of any intelligence should want to stay in the armed forces. This came as a shock to me. That a great dignitary and a famous man, at least locally, was anti the military.[13]

In the light of Foot's comments, Fowles saw for the first time that he might be better suited to university, and enrolled at Oxford to study French, graduating in 1950.

Oxford introduced him to a wealth of new ideas, and prompted him to begin work on *The Aristos*, the collection of aphorisms alluded to earlier. First published in 1964, *The Aristos* was reissued in revised form four years later, with a crucial distinction explained at length in the preface. The pre-Socratic philosopher Heraclitus, Fowles tells us there, 'saw mankind divided into a moral and intellectual *élite* (the *aristoi*, the good ones, *not* – this is a later sense – the ones of noble birth) and an unthinking, conforming mass – *hoi polloi*'. The distinction, Fowles argues, is a crucial one, for in

> every field of human endeavour it is obvious that most of the achieve-
> ments, most of the great steps forward have come from individuals –
> whether they be scientific or artistic geniuses, saints, revolutionaries,
> what you will. And we do not need the evidence of intelligence
> testing to know conversely that the vast mass of mankind are not
> highly intelligent – or highly moral, or highly gifted artistically, or
> indeed highly qualified to carry out any of the nobler human activi-
> ties. (9)

Here it might seem that Fowles has exchanged the dichotomy between the bullied and the bullying, familiar to him from school, or between officers and enlisted men familiar from the Marines, for one that discriminates between the intelligent and gifted on the one hand, and the unintelligent and ungifted on the other. In the remainder of the preface, however, he is at pains to emphasise that the Many should not be regarded with contempt, as the bullied are by the bullying, or as enlisted men may be by their officers. For the distinction between the Few and the Many is '*biologically* irrefutable' (9), he says, and should not be to taken to imply that the Few are superior and the Many inferior. Nor is he interested in any form of government in which the Few dictate to the Many.

Interestingly, this value-free description of the Few and the Many is not to be found in Fowles's comments to an interviewer in the same year that the first edition of *The Aristos* was published. In that year, 1964, he told Roy Newquist, 'I'm against the glamorisation of the Many. I think the common man is the curse of civilisation, not its crowning glory. And he needs education, not adulation.'[14] To this he added, in an article written in the same year, 'I'm sick to death of the inarticulate hero. To hell with the inarticulate. Pity the slobs, but don't glorify them.'[15] The Many are irredeemably unintelligent and insensitive, he suggests here, while the Few are

> pre-eminently creators, not simply highly intelligent or well-informed people; nor people who are simply skilled with words. Such writers can't help being what they are, nor do they cease to belong to the Few if they reject the concept. They are of the Few as this man is born left-handed and this, Chinese. They have no choice about freedom; they have to be free. And this is what isolates them, still, even when all the other barriers between them and the Many, the Profane Mob, are down.[16]

This distinction of Fowles's finds its way into his novels, yet never in such a way that his characters are made to seem black-and-white representatives of one group or the other. Miranda, the girl who is kidnapped in *The Collector*, is one of the Few, for she is intelligent, cultivated and creative – she is an art student, and in a small way, a writer. To say, however, that she is 'of the Few as this man is born left-handed and this, Chinese', and that she (paradoxically) 'has no choice about freedom; [she has] to be free' would be to oversimplify Fowles's presentation of her. For Miranda is Clegg's captive, and in that sense is not free; she is free to write, draw or paint whatever she likes, but in existential terms, she does not enjoy the large measure of freedom that goes with having a clear understanding of who and what she is.

Fowles's interest in French existentialism dates from his undergraduate years at Oxford. He was particularly attracted to the existentialists' views on authenticity and personal freedom. Just as it is important, to him, that sensitive, intelligent men shatter the 'crust' of masculinity, and explore the feminine component within themselves, so under existentialist influence, it also became important that the sensitive and intelligent throw off the shackles of convention freely to discover their authentic selves – the people they really are. 'This', Fowles told James Campbell in 1976, 'is the sort of existential thesis of [my] books – that one has to discover one's [true] feelings.'[17]

We see *how* to discover one's true feelings, and what the significance of this discovery is, in *The Collector*. While in captivity, Miranda scrutinises all her most basic assumptions, and makes some progress towards achieving existential freedom – freedom from the influences of her conventional upbringing – before death cuts her efforts short. As one of the Few, she has the power to change – the power to reach a clearer understanding of herself, and to steer herself in the direction of freedom; Clegg, clearly one of the Many, lacks the power to do either, and is therefore doomed to a life of warped lower middle-class conventionality. His fascination for the reader lies in the fact not that he is unintelligent and insensitive (though he is both), but that Fowles does such a superb job of revealing the horrors of his twisted thinking. '[W]e must', Fowles has said, 'create a society in which the Many will allow the Few to live authentically, *and* to teach and help the Many themselves to begin to do so as well... *The Collector* is a sort of putting of the question'[18] – the question of how to bring that society about.

This question is posed, and the conflict between the Few and the Many enacted, in much of Fowles's fiction. In 'Poor Koko', for example, one of the stories in *The Ebony Tower* (1974), a rather precious man of letters is tied up by a burglar and made to watch as the intruder burns his latest manuscript, page by page. What emerges from this confrontation is a high degree of puzzlement on the part of the man of letters as to why the burglar committed this seemingly gratuitous act of destruction. It is from such puzzlement as this, Fowles suggests, that a better society may emerge – one in which the Few and the Many strive to understand each other better.

Unfortunately, matters are complicated by the fact that the Many are for the most part inarticulate, and have difficulty explaining themselves to the Few. In *The Collector*, Clegg strives in vain to make himself understood to Miranda, just as the burglar in 'Poor Koko' is an enigma to the man of letters. Similarly, in Fowles's most recent novel, *A Maggot*, Rebecca Lee, as clear a representative of the Many as any of his characters, reveals that she is possessed of special knowledge deriving from what may have been a profound religious experience, an incident that she cannot describe to the satisfaction of the solicitor Ayscough. Though language is supposed to be an instrument of communication, it separates the Few from the Many, here and elsewhere in Fowles's fiction, instead of bringing them together.

Fowles often provides his main characters – some of whom number amongst the Many or the existentially inauthentic – with mentors to help them understand life better. In *The Magus*, Nicholas Urfe finds himself under the tutelage of the mysterious Mr Conchis, and in a different way, under that of his girlfriend Alison. An Australian too frank and impatient of pretence to allow herself to be shackled by British social convention, Alison is one of the most authentic characters in the novel. Though neither a writer nor an artist, and in that sense not one of the Few, she nevertheless has a significant influence on Nicholas's search for existential authenticity.

Significantly, Fowles conceals her thoughts from us by making Urfe a first-person narrator, unable to enter her mind. Similarly, in *The French Lieutenant's Woman*, Fowles provides us with generous access to Charles Smithson's mind, but not to the mind of Sarah Woodruff, who acts in part as a mentor and in part as a siren figure. Again, in *Daniel Martin*, which is written partly in the first person and partly in the third, Fowles conceals the thoughts of his main character's mentor, a woman named Jane, not only from the main character, Daniel Martin, but also from the reader.

We can none of us know what goes on in the minds of other people, and for that reason, neither the continuing dialogue of the Few and the Many, nor that of men and women, will lead to any final conclusions about the nature and meaning of life. And this is perhaps the thing that most attracts readers of Fowles to his novels – the sense he gives us that we live in a complex world which can never be fully understood. Fowles presents this idea in existential terms initially, though he is careful to feature only the concept of authenticity in his novels, and takes care not to clutter them with existential terminology, apparently in recognition of the possibility that this might alienate readers. Indeed, so little reference is made to existentialism in his novels that we are not surprised to find Fowles commenting to an interviewer in 1964 that 'A very existentialist novelist... is Jane Austen. Most of the time she was writing about a moral tradition, attempting to establish what authenticity was in her particular world and circumstances.'[19]

It is the concept of authenticity that is central to Fowles's novels, and not existentialism as such. The fact that Fowles's interest in existentialism began to wane in the 1970s, to a point where most of the stories in *The Ebony Tower* are critical of its value as a philosophy, may suggest that his subsequent works are very different. But this is not the case: *The Ebony Tower* stories raise major questions about authenticity, while the novel that follows it, *Daniel Martin*, returns once again to the importance of achieving authenticity. On the other hand, the stories broaden the scope of the central question that features in all of Fowles's novels – the question not only of who and what I really am, but of what *the world* is really like. We may struggle to answer these questions in any number of ways, but we will not succeed, for such questions are notoriously unanswerable. Yet they are questions central to life as we know it, and as we read Fowles's novels, one of the joys we experience is that of speculating on the questions he raises, even though we know that definitive answers can never be found.

2

The Collector

During the fifties Fowles wrote the first drafts of several novels, including *The Collector* and *The Magus*. He completed work on *The Collector* first because, in his own words, 'it seemed more immediately publishable'; the other novels 'were too large and I hadn't the technique'.[1] *The Collector* was accepted for publication in July 1962, and appeared in 1963.[2] Fowles has said that the story line for the novel was suggested to him partly by Bartók's *Bluebeard*, and partly by a contemporary news story of a young man who abducted a girl and kept her prisoner in an air-raid shelter.[3] The news item was, however, only a point of departure for Fowles: Clegg and Miranda differ markedly from their real-life counterparts, not least in that each provides a written account of the abduction, in which the question of existential authenticity plays an important part.

Clegg's account begins before Miranda's and resumes after it, surrounding and containing her narrative as a counterpart to her captivity. Fowles had originally submitted the two narratives in sequence, but made the change on the advice of his editor.[4] Of Miranda, he has said that 'she is an existentialist heroine although she doesn't know it. She is groping for her own authenticity, [her own sense of self-knowledge]. Her tragedy is that she will never live to achieve it. Her triumph is that one day she would have done so.'[5] Clegg writes of her capture, incarceration and death; in contrast to hers, his narrative is an attempt not to understand his behaviour but to justify it to himself. His kidnapping of Miranda, Fowles has commented, is the result of 'a bad education, a mean environment, being orphaned: all factors over which he had no control. In [*The Collector*], I tried to establish the virtual *innocence* of the Many' (*The Aristos*, 10).

If he were a member of the Few, the moral, intellectual and cultural élite that Fowles describes in *The Aristos*, Clegg would have the oppor-

tunity to become existentially authentic because he would have the
intelligence and self-awareness to enable him to do so. Irretrievably one
of the Many, the unintelligent, uncultured mass, he has the innocence
of a man who lacks what it takes to triumph over his background.
Where Miranda's failure to achieve existential authenticity is in
Fowles's estimation 'tragic', Clegg's inability to better himself, despite
the fact that he has certain redeeming features, is pathetic, though the
pathos of his situation gives rise to intriguing moral complexity.

The Collector is correspondingly complex in form: though a self-
consciously realistic novel, its many allusions to Shakespeare's *The
Tempest* take it into the realm of romance; its allusions to Jane Austen's
Emma into the realm of the novel of manners; and its concern with
authenticity into that of the existential novel. For 'the surface "feel" of
the book' Fowles has said that he went to 'that supreme master of the
fake biography, Defoe.'[6] Interestingly, Miranda's narrative, though
reminiscent of a number of Defoe's fictions, has most in common with
Robinson Crusoe, his tale of a sailor marooned on a desert island.
Miranda describes both her captor and her underground cell in Defoe-
like detail (her diary puts us in mind of the journal Crusoe keeps), and
she disrupts the surface realism of the early part of her account in an
effort to persuade herself, as Crusoe does, that, thanks to Providence,
everything will work out for the best.

It is a measure of her initial inauthenticity that she is unable to face
up to the true nature of her predicament. Thus, when Clegg says that
his first name is Ferdinand, she links that name and her own (as various
critics have shown) to Shakespeare's *The Tempest*, and in the absence of
a Prospero with the magical power to ensure a happy ending to the
story of her kidnapping, assumes Prospero's role herself. Unable to
perform magic, she nevertheless assumes superiority over Clegg by
assigning him the part of Caliban, Shakespeare's would-be rapist, and
treats him with the same combination of contempt and kindness as
Prospero does in the play. Just as Shakespeare's Prospero teaches
Caliban to speak, so Miranda corrects Clegg's spoken English; where
Shakespeare's magician-courtier attempts to civilise Caliban, Fowles's
captive seeks to show Clegg, snobbishly, 'how decent human beings live
and behave' (139).

Miranda is initially an unquestioning product of her class and background. As Fowles observes in his Preface to *The Aristos*, she is 'arrogant
in her ideas, a prig, a liberal-humanist snob, like so many university
students' (10). For much of the novel she is disdainful of Clegg's

outlook and opinions, in spite of the fact that he bests her from time to time in debate. At one point she comments, significantly, that her account of their conversations is not altogether accurate. 'I'm cheating', she confesses. 'I didn't say all these things – but I'm going to write what I want to say as well as what I did [say]' (142). Repeatedly we find her saying one thing but doing another: she argues vociferously in favour of pacifism, but is nevertheless prepared to hit Clegg with an axe while attempting to escape. The discrepancy is not lost on her kidnapper: '"I thought pacifists didn't believe in hurting people", he said. I just shrugged and lit a cigarette. I was trembling' (150).

Yet Miranda is not entirely self-deceived. Rather than dismiss Clegg altogether, she is willing to concede that he has his good points: she sees that he differs from Shakespeare's Caliban in his exercise of sexual self-restraint, and she marvels at his apparently boundless generosity. 'It's like having a perpetual Christmas Day', she says in acknowledgement of the clothes, books and other presents he brings her, 'and not even having to thank Santa Claus' (181). It is significant that she feels under no obligation to thank her kidnapper for the gifts: she neglects to do so partly because he is holding her by force, but also because she believes him to be her social and intellectual inferior, undeserving of courtesy. She is careless of his feelings, arrogantly assuming that he has none. 'I could scream abuse at him all day long; he wouldn't mind at all' (171), she says, clearly forgetting her resolution to teach him civilised behaviour by way of example.

As part of her attempt to write herself into a story with a happy ending, Miranda condescendingly tells Clegg a fairy tale – a version of 'Beauty and the Beast', in which the Beast is transformed into a handsome prince the moment he gives his captive princess her freedom – and is surprised that it hurts his feelings. Anxious to be fair to him, while at the same time maintaining the fiction that all will turn out well, she casts herself in the role of Jane Austen's Emma, and assigns Clegg the part of Mr Elton. '[I'll] be like Emma', she fantasises, 'and arrange a marriage for him, and with happier results. Some little Harriet Smith, with whom he could be mousy and sane and happy' (224).

Unfortunately for Miranda, Clegg is more complex than she gives him credit for being. In her efforts to view him fairly she develops a bond of sympathy with him, and mistakenly grants him the civilised restraint of a prince in a fairy tale. She imagines that if she offers to go to bed with him, his undesirable characteristics will melt away magically, and 'Prince Charming [will] step out' (246). What she fails to see is

that Clegg has exercised sexual self-restraint – has behaved not as
Caliban, but as Ferdinand or Prince Charming – only for as long as he
has been able to respect her. When she seeks to seduce him, Miranda
cheapens herself in his eyes by making herself as available as any prostitute. In the event, Clegg is impotent and, racked with humiliation,
begins to treat her cruelly for the first time. He forces her to pose for
pornographic photographs, and later refuses to accept that she is ill
when in fact she has pneumonia. Miranda's inauthenticity – her insist-
ence on fictionalising her situation rather than facing up to its brute
reality – leads not to the happy outcome she fantasises about, but
instead to her death.

Her memories of a relationship with a fortyish London artist,
George Paston (G.P.), reinforce her snobbish tendencies, but ultimately
help her to arrive at a clearer understanding of herself. Anyone interested in being a real artist, G.P. believes, must 'cauterise' their background, and forge authentic values of their own. 'If you're suburban',
writes Miranda, recalling her conversations with him, '(as I realise
D[addy] and M[ummy] are – their laughing at suburbia is just a blind),
you throw away (cauterise) the suburbs... because class is primitive and
silly' (153–4). For G.P. there is no contradiction between maintaining
this view of the class system and openly despising people of a lower
social class.

Clegg, of course, is lower middle class, and by virtue of having won
a huge amount of money on the pools, is newly wealthy. It is under
Paston's influence that Miranda writes: 'I hate all ordinary dull little
people who aren't ashamed of being dull and little. I hate what G.P.
calls the New People, the new-class people with their cars and their
money and their tellies and their stupid vulgarities and their stupid
crawling imitation of the bourgeoisie' (218). Miranda's dealings with
Clegg convince her that she is one of 'the few' (217).[7] What she fails to
recognise is that to be a member of that élite one must accept the faults
of 'the many' and try to diminish them by way of patient, unpatron-
ising education.

Though Paston has a bad influence on Miranda's view of other
people, his influence on her view of herself is positive and enlarging.
When she asks him to comment on her paintings, he finds fault with
them on the grounds that they are stylistically derivative. '[A] picture',
Miranda remembers him saying, 'is like a window straight through to
your inmost heart. And all you've done here is build a lot of little
windows on to a heart full of other fashionable artists' paintings' (170).

Yet Paston takes pains to encourage her: she has the talent to develop a style of her own, he says, and will be able to put that talent to work once she has come to know herself better. In her quest for self-knowledge, Miranda is inspired by G.P.'s example. Though he has his faults – lechery and bad temper, amongst others – he is not a 'phoney' (230); rather, he is a man with a clear sense of his own identity. If she were familiar with the terminology, Miranda would recognise that Paston is existentially authentic, and that it is a feature of his authenticity that he behaves responsibly in his dealings with her. Paston is attracted to her, and even considers asking her to marry him; however, he recognises that the attraction is largely physical, and that marriage to him would not be in Miranda's best interests. 'You know what I am', he says, 'you know I'm old enough to be your father, I'm not reliable at all. Anyhow, you don't love me' (226).

Miranda is correspondingly honest with herself when she begins to recognise that she resembles a character from fairy tale, romance or the novel of manners far less than she does Anne Frank, whose real-life story ended in death. 'I don't think I believe in God any more', she comments near the end of her narrative. 'It is not only me, I think of all the millions who must have lived like this in the war. The Anne Franks. And back through history. What I feel I know now is that God doesn't intervene. He lets us suffer' (233). Having accepted that there is no help to be had from God, and no possibility of drawing on Prospero-like magical powers to end her captivity or transform Clegg from beast to prince, Miranda finds herself in the existentialist position of having to rely entirely on her own resources.

Fortunately, she has by this time come to know herself better and to feel increasingly confident of her ability to cope. 'I pick up my old self', she comments, 'and I see it's silly. A toy I've played with too often' (257). That former self, she adds, 'consisted of things older people had taught me. All the mud of their stale ideas on the shoe of me' (258). With a clearer idea of who she is, Miranda is near to achieving existential authenticity; but although she speaks of having found a new self within herself that Clegg 'can never win against' (258) – a self that, were she released, would help her to lead a freer and more satisfying life – the opportunity to live that life is denied her. Like Anne Frank, she dies before her time; she suffers physical defeat on the brink of psychological triumph.

Clegg's narrative, too, is allied to Defoe, though less closely to *Robinson Crusoe* than to *Moll Flanders*, a book he makes no mention of

Violence, no guilt, inauthenticity.

having read. Like Moll, Clegg presents us with a retrospective account of his wrongdoings, and at times seems sorry for what he has done. But again like Moll, he cannot resist supplying us with a largely self-congratulatory account of his crime. 'I thought of everything', he says at one point, 'just like I'd been doing it all my life. Like I'd been a secret agent or a detective' (25). It is a sign of his existential inauthenticity that Clegg identifies with the secret agents and detectives he has read about in mass-market novels. Where such fictional characters kill people without a moment's hesitation, Clegg has a murky awareness that in contributing to Miranda's death, he has committed a dreadful crime, and seeks, as Moll does, to deflect our sense of outrage. Seeing her dead, he says, 'I finally forgave her [for repeatedly treating me conde-scendingly]' (281); later, he thinks of killing himself, so that he and Miranda might be buried side by side, like romantic lovers who decided to die together, rather than live, either of them, separate from the other. This, however, is only a passing fancy: Clegg loves life too much to kill himself, and chillingly, finds that he can carry on without Miranda without feeling too much grief or guilt.

At the beginning of her narrative, Moll Flanders draws attention to her disadvantaged background – to the fact that she never knew her father, and was deserted by her mother while still a small child. Similarly, Clegg points out that he was only two when his father died, and that his mother left him to be brought up by his Aunt Annie and Uncle Dick. For a time, he tells us, Dick took the place of his dead father, encouraging his interest in, for example, fishing and butterfly-collecting; however, he died when Clegg was fifteen. Like Moll, who says that she entered a life of crime because she had no one to provide the guidance and help she needed, Clegg is careful to emphasise that when he kidnapped Miranda, 'I was all on my own... I had no one to turn to' (273).

Moll says that when she committed her first act of theft, 'I am very sure I had no manner of design in my head when I went out, I neither knew or consider'd where to go, or on what business'.[8] Clegg comments, similarly, that when he first went to look at the house that he later buys with his football pool winnings, 'I didn't go... with the intention of seeing whether there was anywhere to [imprison someone]. I can't really say what intention I had' (18). And where Moll claims that she is not really responsible for her criminal acts, since most were committed at the prompting of the Devil, Clegg speaks of being subject to forces beyond his control – of being 'swept on, like down rapids, I might hit something, I might get through' (26).

Inauthentic · Identity

Clegg's refusal to accept responsibility for his actions is another indication that he is existentially inauthentic. Still another is his tendency to view his experiences in the light of his reading – a tendency he shares with Miranda, though his reading is much more limited in scope. Throughout her imprisonment, Clegg refuses to let Miranda have news of the outside world, having learned from a book entitled *Secrets of the Gestapo* that Nazi interrogators 'didn't let the prisoners know anything,... so they were cut off from their old world. And that broke them down' (44). It is obviously with this book in mind that he tells Miranda, shortly after her arrival, that he is 'only obeying orders' (32); and says, addressing the reader, that the kidnapping is like 'doing something in enemy territory' (30). Similarly, his pre-kidnapping fantasy about rescuing Miranda from an attacker, which gives way to a fantasy in which he is himself the attacker, probably derives from the pornographic fiction he mentions reading. And although Clegg seems not to be acquainted with Shakespeare's *The Tempest* – the Ferdinand-Miranda coincidence has to be pointed out to him – he mentions Romeo and Juliet by name near the end of his narrative, when he daydreams about killing himself and trying to make his death and Miranda's appear to be a suicide pact.

It is a further sign of Clegg's inauthenticity that he makes extensive use of clichés and euphemisms. Such phrases as 'as they say', 'as you might say', and 'in my humble opinion' (linking him with Dickens's Uriah Heep) appear with great frequency in his narrative, as do such euphemisms as 'woman of the streets' for prostitute, 'artistic' for obscene and 'passed away' for died.[9] Miranda shrewdly observes that Clegg's accent, vocabulary and attitudes are those of his austerely respectable, lower middle-class Aunt Annie. 'You have money', Miranda tells Clegg, '[and] you aren't stupid, you could become whatever you liked. Only you've got to shake off the past. You've got to kill your aunt and the house you lived in and the people you lived with. You've got to become a new human being' (82). Unfortunately for Miranda, becoming 'a new human being' – an existentially authentic individual whose language bespeaks the assurance of self-knowledge – is out of the question for Clegg.

Prior to the kidnapping, Clegg tries to remake himself in Miranda's image. 'I began to... read the classy newspapers', he says, '[and] I went to the National Gallery and the Tate... I didn't enjoy them much, ...But I went so as I could talk to her, so I wouldn't seem ignorant' (17). Clegg's problem is partly that he has the wrong background and attitudes to appreciate either the better newspapers or the paintings exhibited at major galleries. Moreover, he lacks the self-awareness of a sane man: amongst other things, he is unable to see that if he truly loved Miranda, he would not imprison her in a cellar. 'What I fear in you', says Miranda at one point, 'is something you don't know is in you' (75). That 'something' is his seemingly limitless fund of resentment against a world that has made him feel ashamed of his class and accent.

Unlike Miranda, who moves towards a greater understanding of herself as she writes, Clegg seeks only to excuse his behaviour. A typically inauthentic character, he claims to have acted at the prompting of forces beyond his control. 'I took a risk', he says at one point, 'perhaps I wanted to give fate a chance to stop me' (26); elsewhere, he comments that I was 'being drawn on against my will' (107). After the humiliation of being found impotent, however, he speaks as though he were free of 'paying [Miranda] back for all the things she said and thought about me' (118), and excuses his cruelty to her on the grounds that 'I was acting for the best and within my rights' (125). Similarly, he excuses taking photographs of her in her underwear with the comment that 'I'm not really that sort and I was only like it that night because of all that happened and the strain I was under' (95). Near the end of his narrative he says that he failed to secure medical help for her because he 'wasn't to know that she was really ill' (271), and because, in any case, '[a] doctor could have done little good, in my opinion. [She] was too far gone' (286).

Clegg is unaware of the self-contradiction not only in these last two statements, but in his comment that when Miranda died, 'I knelt and said a prayer, ...not that I believe in religion, but it seemed right' (281). Though he rejects belief in God ('I think we are just insects, we live a bit and then die and that's the lot. There's no mercy in things. There's not even a Great Beyond. There's nothing' [284]), he sees no contradiction in observing a religious ritual. He accepts the basic existential principle that he lives in a world bereft of God; yet he clings, inauthentically, to the forms of religion, lacking the initiative and ability to forge any but the most selfish value system of his own. Unlike Miranda, who finds inner strength in the course of her ordeal, Clegg remains pathetically weak. 'You don't know what you are', he says to her at one point. 'You're everything. I got nothing if you go' (262).

Fowles's comment that the kidnapping of Miranda is the result of 'a bad education, a mean environment, being orphaned: all factors over which [Clegg] had no control' (Preface to *The Aristos*, 10) implies that with a good education, a better environment and a happier family background, the kidnapper might have been quite different. Yet a world in which such conditions would prevail remains for Fowles a Utopian fantasy. Miranda's attempts to re-educate Clegg are in vain: he is too much a product of his background to believe, for example, that art should be anything but strictly representational, and this attitude firmly prevents him from appreciating modern painting. Moreover, Clegg succeeds only in perverting her comments. After developing his nude photos of her, he comments that the best of them 'were when she stood in her high heels, from the back. The tied hands to the bed made what they call an interesting motif' (122). 'An interesting motif' is, of course, Miranda's phrase; it is unaccompanied by any sense of the horror of what he has done.

It is significant that we end *The Collector* with a sense that Clegg is ineducable, for there is evidence to suggest that Fowles shares Miranda's snobbery more fully than he would care to admit. Midway through her narrative, Miranda comments that '[t]he ordinary man is the curse of civilisation' (137); while, only a year after *The Collector* was published, Fowles told Roy Newquist, similarly, that in his opinion, 'the common man is the curse of civilisation, not its crowning glory'.[10] In *The Magus*, a novel Fowles was writing at about the same time as *The Collector*, but which was published several years after it, the seemingly ineducable common man is conspicuous by his absence. *The Magus* focuses not on the common man but instead on a public school-cum-Oxford product, Nicholas Urfe, who works toward achieving existential authenticity under the tutelage of a Prospero-like figure, the mysterious Maurice Conchis.

3

The Magus

The success of *The Collector* gave Fowles the confidence to return to the novels he had begun in the fifties, with a view to revising them for publication. He soon found that *The Magus*, a novel he had already put through 'countless transformations', demanded precedence over the others.[1] In 1964 he began collating and rewriting all the earlier drafts, and completed what he thought was to be the final draft, which was published in the following year. When the book came out, however, he was dissatisfied with it:

> I well remember receiving the first bound copy, opening it at hazard, and seeing a flagrantly unnecessary word in the very first sentence my eyes lighted on; then a clumsy repetition a few lines down – four or five bungles on just that one page. I knew I had committed a very ancient literary crime. Obsessed with story, I had neglected its articulation. I had published before I was ready.[2]

Dissatisfaction prompted rewriting, and in 1977 Fowles brought out a more polished version of *The Magus* – a version, in addition, whose sex scenes are more explicit than the original's, and whose ending is less ambiguous.[3]

Given that a magus is a magician, sorcerer or wise man, a reader coming to *The Magus* for the first time might imagine that Maurice Conchis, the magus of the title, is a man with supernatural powers. If such a reader were also to be told that the novel's seventy-eight chapters correspond to the seventy-eight cards in the Tarot deck, used in fortune-telling, he or she might wonder whether Conchis has the power of prophecy.[4] In fact, however, Conchis is only a secondary character in the novel – the main character being a young man named Nicholas Urfe – and like Urfe, he is possessed of no more than ordinary human powers. If, Conchis believes, it is wise to do anything in a world too complex to yield its mysteries to human investigation, it is to strive towards an ultimately unattainable goal – existential authenticity.

The fact that the novel's chapter structure corresponds to the seventy-eight cards of the Tarot deck illustrates one of Fowles's most important points in the novel. Living in an existential world – a world that is infinitely complex, and therefore ultimately unknowable – we have two choices. We can spend our lives struggling with a wide variety of bewildering epistemological, metaphysical and ethical questions, aware that we will never be able to answer them with absolute certainty. Alternatively, we can choose the security of an established order – the certainty afforded by a religion or the occult, for example – in the interests of reducing complexity and uncertainty to a spurious but comprehensible clarity.

To read *The Magus* as a novel that extols the wisdom of the Tarot deck is to misread it, for Fowles does not wish to claim that the occult tells us everything we need to know about our ultimately unknowable world. Instead, he wants to suggest that his novel is an ordered counterpart to the ordered, simplified image of the world that we create for the purposes of everyday living. *The Magus* is, of course, structured in ways that the world is not; but its structure is merely a convenience, a matter of making the novel accessible to the reader, just as grouping stars into constellations helps us to give order to the endless profusion of heavenly bodies. Ultimately, the novel has no more 'real signifi-cance', as Fowles says in the foreword, 'than that of the Rorschach test in psychology. Its meaning is whatever reaction it provokes in the reader, and so far as I am concerned there is no given "right" reaction' (8). Unlike the constellations, whose identity we all agree on, *The Magus* is meant to be a novel of such complexity that it gives rise to as many interpretations as there are readers.

Urfe involves the reader in reliving the frustration he felt in trying to make sense of his experiences both in England and on the (fictional) Greek island of Phraxos.[5] The novel's main character is, Fowles says in his foreword, 'a typical inauthentic man of the 1945–50 period'[6] – the kind of man who plays a role, or series of roles, in life, because he does not know who he really is. Urfe's role-playing makes it impossible for him to view the world clearly and come to grips with the problems it presents. As we read the novel, however, we see him shed these roles and come to a clearer understanding not only of who he is but of the kind of world he inhabits. While individual readers may disagree about other aspects of the novel, there is consensus about the ending: by the time he has reached it, Urfe has made significant progress towards becoming existentially authentic.

Writing in the first person, Urfe begins by telling us about his time at Oxford and his membership in 'Les Hommes Révoltés', a student club devoted to the study of existentialism. Here he learns about the distinction between authentic and inauthentic behaviour, and is quick to condemn other people – in particular, his parents – for being inauthentic. For it is clear to Urfe that his father merely plays the role of a high-ranking professional soldier, and his mother that of a model wife. When his parents die in a plane crash, Urfe feels 'a sense of relief, of freedom', for he now has 'no family to trammel what I regarded as my real self' (16).

In retrospect, however, he can see that at this point in his life, his understanding of existential theory was flawed. He and the other members of his club talked endlessly, he says, about

> being and nothingness and called a certain inconsequential behaviour 'existentialist'. Less enlightened people would have called it capricious or just plain selfish; but we didn't understand that the heroes, or anti-heroes, of the French existentialist novels we read were not supposed to be realistic. We tried to imitate them, mistaking metaphorical descriptions of complex modes of feeling for straightforward prescriptions of behaviour. (17)

Despite his professed interest in discovering his 'real self'(16), Urfe spends his undergraduate years turning his imperfect knowledge of existentialism not to understanding himself better, but to seducing women. His 'technique' at this time was, he says, to behave like the existential heroes he had read about, and 'make a show of unpredictability, cynicism, and indifference'. Then, 'like a conjurer with his white rabbit, I produced the solitary heart' (21). Urfe's technique is as carefully rehearsed as a conjurer's act. Once he has seduced the woman in question, he loses interest in her: 'There were sometimes a few tedious weeks of letters, but I soon put the solitary heart away, "assumed responsibility with my total being" and showed the Chesterfieldian mask instead' (21).

Only in retrospect does he see that he was perverting existentialism to his own ends, and that in doing this he was mistaken. 'I mistook the feeling of relief that dropping a girl always brought for a love of [existential] freedom' (21). At time of writing the narrative, he confesses that he spent his university years donning a series of inauthentic 'masks', masks that concealed his true identity not only from the women he seduced, but also from the existentalist he was supposed to be – the man in search of his 'real self'. Ultimately it becomes clear to him that what he took to be 'freedom' was in fact a form of shameless self-deception.

The English, says Urfe on the subject of self-deception, are 'born with masks and bred to lie' (372). In context he means that, in class-conscious England, members of the middle and upper classes acquire a socially acceptable accent and set of manners, and learn to conceal their true feelings not only from others but from themselves as well. In first describing Alison Kelly, the young Australian he meets in London before leaving for Greece, Urfe's snobbery comes to the fore. Her voice, he says, 'only very slightly Australian, yet not English, veered between harshness, faint nasal rancidity, and a strange salty directness' (24). So far as Urfe is concerned, the 'harshness' of Alison's accent is one of many signs that Australians are socially inferior, and deserve to be treated badly, especially if they are women. Alison's 'waif-like' (23) appearance and 'characteristic bruised look' only make him 'want to bruise her more' (31).

As their affair is drawing to what Urfe takes to be its end, he ungallantly tells a friend in London that he has remained with her only because she is 'cheaper than central heating' (36); later, on Phraxos, he reflects that if he misses her, it is a matter of 'sexual frustration, not regretted love' (54). For her part, Alison suspects that Urfe will never marry her because he considers her to be 'a whore and a colonial' (35). Yet the 'strange salty directness' (24) in her voice suggests to him that she may be more sincere than his English friends; moreover, he is impressed by the fact that she is 'crude but alive' (26), and that unlike his other conquests, she 'didn't fall for the solitary heart; she had a nose for emotional blackmail' (35). Socially unacceptable Alison may be, but she is also more direct, more energetic and more honest than any English girl Urfe has ever known. Though he leaves her with a sense that 'she [had] loved me more than I loved her, and that consequently I had in some indefinable way won' (48), he is nevertheless drawn back to her by the qualities he admires. On Phraxos, these qualities appeal to Urfe when he is treated to a dose of his own medicine by a young Englishwoman who deliberately plays on *his* affections.

It is Conchis, of course, who introduces him to the woman concerned, a woman known to him first as Lily, then Julie. But the lessons she has to teach him are not the only ones he has to learn, for Conchis is aware that the young man will only begin to behave well to women when he attains to greater self-knowledge. Prior to meeting Conchis, Urfe has been wrongly diagnosed as having syphilis, and has considered, then rejected the idea of committing suicide. It was 'a Mercutio death I was looking for, not a real one', he comments. 'I was putting on an act for the benefit of someone, [when] this action could be done only if it was spontaneous, pure – and moral' (62). Urfe sees all too clearly that his suicide would be no more than playacting – that he is, was, and unless he does something about it, always will be, 'intensely false; in existentialist terms, inauthentic' (62).

Significantly, Conchis does not make use of existential terminology in the novel, for he knows that to do so would only encourage Urfe in his 'playacting'. Yet it is in the interests of guiding him towards greater self-knowledge that he tells the young man four stories, each of them auto-biographical. Conchis' first story concerns his desertion from the army during the First World War; he tells it not as a tale of shameful cowardice but as a triumph of personal integrity. The war, he says, was a 'barbarous crime of civilisation, [a] terrible human lie' (128), and to remain fighting in it would have been to betray his 'true self' (152). Conchis' fiancée, Lily, tries to persuade him to return to the front, but her arguments are based on hopelessly conventional notions of bravery, duty and honour which only those who have not been involved in the fighting can take seriously. 'To thine own self be true' is the text of Conchis' lesson – even when it means running counter to strongly held conventional opinion.

We can see this more clearly in his third story, which concerns Henrik Nygaard, a hermit he encountered while doing research on birds in the high Arctic. Nygaard, a strict Jansenist, seems to Conchis to be trying to achieve a union with God; but one evening, as he listens to the hermit crying in the wilderness, he concludes that the latter has been communing with Him for some time. 'He was not waiting to meet God', he says of Nygaard. 'He was meeting God; and had been meeting [Him] probably for many years. He was not waiting for some certainty. He lived in it' (308). Later, however, Conchis revises this statement, hinting that Nygaard's experience may be incomplete: the hermit may not have succeeded in finding God, but 'he had the Holy Spirit' (309), nevertheless.

Given Conchis' lack of religious convictions, the Nygaard story is a statement not about seeking God, but about seeking oneself – a statement that is best understood in the context of Fowles's longstanding interest in Jung.[7] Central to Jungian theory is the process of individuation – the process by which the conscious and unconscious elements of an individual's mind interact to achieve a new psychic balance. The final stage of it – the stage at which there emerges into consciousness an inner personality otherwise hidden from the individual, the self – is best compared, Jung tells us, to a profound religious experience,

> a change of feeling similar to that... [of] a father to whom a son has been born, a change known to us from the testimony of St Paul: 'Yet not I, but Christ liveth in me'. The symbol 'Christ' as 'son of man' is an analogous psychic experience of a higher spiritual being who is invisibly born in the individual...[8]

Jung also says that the endpoint of the process is akin to discovering 'God within us', and emphasises that the self is 'an unknowable essence' whose totality we cannot understand, since it 'transcends our powers of comprehension'.[9] Thus the point that Conchis is making about Nygaard, however obliquely, is that the hermit has a sense of his true self – an imperfect sense, perhaps, bearing in mind that 'if he still lacked God, he had the Holy Spirit' (309) – but a sense of it just the same. In Conchis' opinion, Nygaard is to be envied, for even this kind of limited self-knowledge eludes the vast majority of people.

His second story concerns a wealthy nobleman named de Deukans, who took an interest in Conchis as a young man. There is an obvious parallel to be drawn between de Deukans' relationship with Conchis and Conchis' relationship with Urfe, as well as a further, more important parallel that escapes the young man's attention. What Urfe fails to see is that de Deukans stands in relation to Conchis, and Conchis to Urfe, in much the same way as God to humanity. Conchis is careful to point out that the role he assumes in the masque, or 'godgame', he creates for Urfe, is at times the role of God, but he is careful to issue a disclaimer.[10] 'You must not think I know every answer', he emphasises to the young man, 'for I do not' (185). Whatever Urfe may think, the fact remains that Conchis is human and fallible; he is not an omniscient God. Nor is he omnipotent: when Conchis says that the events in our lives are governed not by a divine Providence, but by 'hazard' (186), or chance, he is hinting that he is unable to control the godgame's script. How Urfe will reply to what is said to him in the course of the game, how he will behave when certain things happen – all this and more will be a matter of chance rather than design, and be part of a changing rather than a predetermined script.

Just as important to the godgame as Conchis' disclaimers about his omniscience and omnipotence is the question that de Deukans puts to him, and that Conchis puts in turn to Urfe: 'Which are you drinking? The water or the wave?' It is, Conchis comments, a question that 'should always be asked. It is not a precept. But a mirror' (188). What the question calls on Urfe to do is to distinguish between the general and the particular – between water, which has been present on Earth since the beginning of time, and the individual wave, formed by the wind and brought to an end in the time it takes to reach the shore. Conchis poses this question so that Urfe might ask himself why he is attracted first to Alison, then to Julie. Is it simply that each is a nubile young woman, an object of lust? Or is he drawn to them because, in addition to being physically attractive, each has a strikingly unique outlook and personality?

The fact is, of course, that Urfe is attracted to both the particular *and* the general, though less to the 'wave' – the individual – than to the 'water', the female sex. The question Conchis poses is a 'mirror' in the sense that it reflects Urfe's belief, at the beginning of the novel, that women are sex objects, and this, of course, is a revealing aspect of his existential inauthenticity. If he is to become more authentic, Urfe must make sense of the world in his own way. Conchis presents his question about the water or the wave not as a 'precept' – a behest to Urfe to value the individual more highly than the general – for to view the world as Conchis does would mean living by another man's view of it, instead of formulating his own. The existentially authentic individual must construct the world for himself in his own way.

It is a sign of Urfe's longstanding inauthenticity that he fails to recognise how genuine a person Alison is. By the time she has been in touch to suggest that they spend some time together either on Phraxos or in Athens, Urfe has met Julie, and has become so attracted to what he takes to be her superior charms that Alison's invitation seems an intrusion. Having the latter visit the island is 'unthinkable' (203): Urfe is anxious not to have Julie, who is of his own class and background, meet an Australian girlfriend who is 'half-baked culturally', 'gauche', and in any case someone 'I know I don't love...' (207). He arranges to visit Alison at a safe remove from the island, in Athens; there he tells her that he has syphilis, so that he will be spared the hypocrisy of making love to her. When they spend the night on Parnassus, however, Urfe suddenly realises that he *does* love Alison:

> Suddenly… I felt a passionate wave of desire for her. It was not only lust, not only because she looked, as she did in her periodic fashion, disturbingly pretty, small-breasted, small-waisted, leaning on one hand, dimpled then grave; …but because I was seeing through all the ugly, the unpoetic accretions of modern life to the naked real self of her – a vision of her as naked in that way as she was in body; Eve glimpsed again through ten thousand generations.

> It rushed on me, it was quite simple, I did love her, I wanted to keep her *and* I wanted to keep – or to find – Julie. It wasn't that I wanted one more than the other, I wanted both. I had to have both; there was no emotional dishonesty in it. (269)

Though this passage may seem a step in the direction of existential authenticity for Urfe, it is clear on closer examination that his feelings for both women are in fact inauthentic. Alison attracts him in general terms, as 'water' – as an object of lust and an archetypal female, an 'Eve glimpsed again through ten thousand generations' – but not as 'wave', as an individual in her own right. If asked to comment on her personality, interests and aspirations, he would be obliged to confess that in reality she is a stranger to him.

Similarly, all he really knows about Julie, who has been playing the role of Lily up to now, while largely concealing her own identity, is that she has 'hinted at [being] a girl from a world and background very like my own' (202). To have a relationship with Julie, Urfe comments, would be 'to drink the wave' (202) – experience the individual – but in fact he knows so little about her that he is obliged to confess that she is someone he must set out to 'find' (269). His closing comment in the above passage, that there is 'no emotional dishonesty' in what he says, may be true so far as wanting both of them is concerned, but the fact that he knows Alison only as an archetypal woman, and Julie only as someone from his own class and background, shows that he has not yet made an honest attempt at loving either of them. In his attitude to the two women, he is existentially inauthentic.

Further evidence of Urfe's inauthenticity at this point in the novel is to be found in his descriptions of other characters. Just as Miranda likens Clegg to Caliban in *The Collector*, for the sake of persuading herself that a Prospero-figure will appear to free her from captivity, so Urfe compares Conchis to Prospero, and speaks of 'hoping [to be] Ferdinand' (204), for the sake of assuring himself that he will be united with Julie/Miranda. Elsewhere, Urfe describes Julie as a figure of mystery, as an 'extinct Lawrentian woman of the past, the woman inferior to man in everything, but that one great power of female dark mystery and beauty' (242). Here again he is refusing to see her clearly, as an individual in her own right, but instead as mediated through a haze of preconception.

Moreover, it is clear from his choice of language that his relationship with Julie is only a game to him. The more time he spends with her, the closer he gets to making love to her, so that 'a deep excitement buoyed me on, a knowledge like that of a poker-player who needs only one more card to have an unbeatable hand' (356). Similarly, in describing one of his conversations with Alison, he comments that she 'gave no sign of listening; I produced my trump' (273). With Urfe's game-playing in mind, we are not surprised that the letter he sends Alison, lamenting their break-up, is couched in the kind of hollow language that one of Lawrence's least sincere and most manipulative characters – Gerald or Loerke in *Women in Love*, for example, might use – while Alison's note, to which he is replying, is simple, direct and deflationary:

> Think what it would be like if you got back to your island and there was no old man, no girl any more. No mysterious fun and games. The whole place locked up for ever.
>
> It's finished finished *finished*. (278)

In retrospect, Urfe can see that it is partly her directness – her 'truth-seeking eyes' (246) and rejection of hollow rhetoric – that has attracted him to her all along; but it is not until his time on Phraxos is over that he begins to value these qualities properly.

On his return to the island, Urfe finds himself still very much in love with Alison – so much so that to resume his relationship with Julie seems at first like 'adultery' (283). After only a short time, however, he does resume the relationship, and it continues to be shallow and inauthentic. As before, he compares himself to Ferdinand in *The Tempest*, assigning Conchis the role of Prospero and Julie that of Miranda. He also sees himself as a Theseus figure, caught up in a labyrinthine godgame, with Julie playing the role of Ariadne, and the mysterious black man who has recently come to the island serving as the Minotaur. As an Ariadne figure, Julie has now become a saviour to him – someone who can help him understand the complexities of the godgame and life itself. Later, however, when he learns from her sister June that Julie was once married to a homosexual, Urfe casts her in the role of a 'sleeping princess... not merely in love with me, but erotically starved...' (371), and assigns himself the part of a Prince Charming who will satisfy her every sexual desire.

Urfe's invocation of fairy-tale characters to describe his relationship with Julie suggests not only that he is existentially inauthentic, but that his immaturity is another barrier to his forming sound relationships. Though he comes to know Julie no better than he did before visiting Alison, her sexual attractiveness and shared middle-class background are enough to convince him, on his return to Phraxos, that he has 'been waiting to meet [her] all [his] life' (355). Only a short time later he thinks of Alison, callously, as 'spilt milk; or spilt semen. I wanted Julie ten times more' (387). Conchis puts Urfe's preference for Julie to the test by telling him that Alison has committed suicide, though in fact she has not. At first Urfe feels guilty of the crime of having tried to impose 'the role I needed from Alison on her real self' (400). But with the passing of time, he edges her death 'out of the moral world into the aesthetic, where it was easier to live with', and slips 'from true remorse, to... disguised self-forgiveness' (401).

It is now that Conchis tells him his fourth story, an autobiographical account that indirectly reveals how thoughtless Urfe has been not only in choosing Julie over Alison, but in forgiving himself for making the choice so easily. The story concerns the much more serious choice that Conchis was obliged to make during the war. He tells how, as mayor of a village on an island overrun by the Nazis, he came under the command of a sadistic officer named Wimmel, who forced him to choose between clubbing two resistance fighters to death with a rifle, or, if he failed to do that, bringing about the execution of eighty villagers. It was an impossible choice, and Conchis says that he sacrificed the villagers not because he was indifferent to their fate, but because he was convinced that the exercise of his freedom was 'more important than common sense, self-preservation, yes, than my own life, than the lives of the eighty hostages' (434). For Conchis to have clubbed the two men to death would have been to deny who and what he is – a human being to whom that form of execution is an unconscionable act of barbarism.

Conchis may now have the lives of eighty people on his conscience, but at least he can tell himself that it was not he but the Germans who killed them. The freedom he exercises is, Urfe reflects, 'much older than... existentialist freedom': it is a freedom governed by the 'moral imperative' (441) that we must avoid inflicting unnecessary pain on others. Urfe now begins to realise that he has exercised his own freedom only to satisfy personal desire, and not in the best interests of either Alison or Julie. He grieves for Alison for the first time, and feels guilty that he did not behave more considerately to her when she was alive. Yet his attitude to Julie remains largely unchanged: as before, he is drawn to her Englishness and shared middle-class background, but remains incurious as to what she is like as an individual in her own right. When he makes love to her for the first time, it seems a fulfilment of the existentially inauthentic dream in which he has pictured Julie as a Miranda figure and himself as Ferdinand. But that dream comes abruptly to an end when he is put on trial by Conchis and the others who helped to facilitate the godgame; it is then that the folly of his Miranda-fixation is made clear.

The trial is anything but fair. Urfe is presumed guilty from the outset; he is mocked, humiliated and, perhaps most importantly of all, 'disintoxicated' (555) of Julie, who points out his faults and reveals that her real lover is the young black man named Joe. Though he briefly sees that the Ferdinand/Miranda parallel is more accurately a parallel between himself and Iago, Joe and Othello, Julie and Desdemona, he concludes that turning life 'into fiction, to hold reality away' (539) is ultimately self-defeating. What he must do instead is try to understand himself and the world in which he lives as clearly as possible, without recourse to the distorting lens of fiction. Forced to face the fact that Julie never loved him, he asks himself how she could have played the role of lover without really meaning it. Here, of course, he has forgotten about his own deceitful past, about playing the role of 'conjurer with his white rabbit, [repeatedly producing] the solitary heart' (21) in the interests of enticing women into bed.

With all his illusions collapsed like a house of cards, Urfe thinks once again of Alison, whom he still believes to be dead. Too late (it seems) he realises that her 'special genius, or uniqueness, was her normality, her reality, her predictability; her crystal core of non-betrayal; her attachment to all that [Julie] was not' (553). At first this seems like so much wasted emotion, given that his former girlfriend is no longer alive; but Urfe, now in Athens, glimpses her in the street one evening, and realises that the news of her suicide was just another fiction, another piece in the puzzle of Conchis' godgame. Though he searches everywhere for Alison, wanting to discover the truth about her participation (if any) in the masque Conchis created, Urfe is unable to find her, and finally becomes as 'disintoxicated of her as I was of [Julie]' (565).

On his return to England, he visits Julie's mother, Mrs de Seitas, to see if she knows anything of Alison, and is surprised to discover not only that they have met, but that they have become 'good friends' (598). Mrs de Seitas is not anxious to bring Urfe and Alison together too quickly, however, for she is aware that the former has two lessons to learn about human relations prior to their reunion.[11] The first lesson is that every good relationship is based on truthfulness and trust: Alison, says Mrs de Seitas, has learned this lesson already, and in addition has 'a very rare capacity for attachment and devotion' (601).

The second lesson – that it is important not to inflict unnecessary pain on others – is a lesson that Urfe has still to learn. Whether the godgame is now over is not entirely clear, and for this reason he cannot be certain whether his decision to rent lodgings from a Mrs Kemp, and to have as a non-paying flatmate a street-girl named Jojo, are purely as a matter of chance, or have been engineered by Mrs de Seitas and other members of the 'godgame' team, now returned from Phraxos. Both characters are in any case important to his development: Mrs Kemp serves as a surrogate mother to him, while Jojo provides him with the opportunity to demonstrate (if only to himself) that he is capable of treating another human being with kindness and consideration.

Urfe is kind to Jojo, but in trying to persuade her that what he feels for her is affection rather than desire, convinces her that he feels neither. When she leaves him, he feels a pang of regret: Jojo, he says, was 'the last person in the world I wanted to hurt. It was as if I had kicked a starving mongrel in its poor, thin ribs' (643). This is clearly a step forward for Urfe (we have only to think back to the beginning of the novel, to his many sexual conquests, who are no sooner seduced than abandoned, for this to be evident to us); yet Fowles holds in suspense the question of what will happen in respect of his relationship to Alison.

The two are reunited in the closing pages of the novel. As they meet, Alison gives him a 'lancing look' (647), the same look that Sarah

Woodruff gives Charles in *The French Lieutenant's Woman*.[12] In both novels, the look is partly a challenge, a challenge in this case to Urfe to see if he has learned the two lessons Mrs de Seitas has mentioned. Whether the godgame is over, or whether Conchis and his associates are 'watching' (649) is not clear. There is some suggestion that Urfe is still inauthentic in his descriptions of Alison as a mythological figure, 'come from Tartarus' (648), and as a 'priestess from the Temple of Demeter' (650); for in these descriptions, Urfe is displaying his old habit of seeing Alison not as she is, but instead as she appears to him when mediated through the distorting lens of fantasy.

Yet, apart from this, he makes an unprecedented effort to be honest with her, telling her frankly that, in spite of his 'disintoxication' on Phraxos, he is still not entirely certain of how he feels about Julie. From this it is clear that Urfe has not yet achieved existential authenticity, though he has come a long way from the inauthenticity he displayed at the beginning of the novel. Whether he and Alison will get together again is uncertain, for the revised version of the novel ends in the 'frozen present tense':

> She is silent, she will never speak, never forgive, never reach a hand, never leave this frozen present tense. All waits, suspended. ...A flight of pigeons over the houses; fragments of freedom, hazard, an anagram made flesh. And somewhere the stinging smell of burning leaves. (656)

Fowles concludes *The Magus* with this frozen tableau rather than with a conventional ending that would distort the account he has given of the complexity of human relationships in an existential world. The mention of 'freedom' and 'hazard' reminds us that Urfe must struggle with the anguish of freedom in an infinitely complex world. Yet there is a hint that things will turn out well for Urfe and Alison in the near-Joycean phrase, 'an anagram made flesh' (656).[13] The name 'Alison' is contained as an anagram within the name 'Nicholas', and this suggests that she is an important part of his life – too important, it seems, for him simply to walk away from her.

In the original version of *The Magus*, Urfe does walk away from her: Alison may follow, but then again, she may not. The revised version is less ambiguous. Not only does Urfe remain rather than leave; he confesses to Alison that he will 'never be more than half a human being without [her]' (655). The quotation from Catullus that ends both versions is Fowles's final hint as to its outcome: '*cras amet qui numquam amavit/ quique amavit cras amet*' (656). 'Let him love tomorrow who has never loved/ And he who has loved let him love tomorrow.' Here love is extolled as a virtue, whether one has any experience of it or not: at novel's end we have a sense that Urfe has learned from the 'godgame' something of the complexity and mystery of human relationships, and of the joys of love to come.

4

The French Lieutenant's Woman

Fowles has said that *The French Lieutenant's Woman* arose from an image that came to his mind as he awoke one morning. It was the image of a woman standing at the end of a long quay, her back turned as if in reproach to Victorian society.[1] Though he was writing another novel at the time, he was so taken with the image that he broke off to start a new work of fiction set in England in 1867.

Fowles chose the date carefully. In 1867 John Stuart Mill tried (but failed) to persuade his Parliamentary colleagues to grant women the vote; Mill's efforts are mentioned in the novel, and serve as an appropriate backdrop to its treatment of the lot of the intelligent woman in the mid-nineteenth century. In the same year, Marx published the first volume of *Das Kapital*, a book concerned with social class, an issue that figures importantly in *The French Lieutenant's Woman*. Marx wanted to dedicate that volume to Darwin, perhaps for the sake of acknowledging that his own theory about a strong and numerous proletariat eventually overthrowing a weaker, smaller middle class, was influenced by Darwin's concept of the survival of the fittest.

Mill, Marx and Darwin had a significant impact on nineteenth-century thinking, and have continued to be influential in our own century. Yet in *The French Lieutenant's Woman* Fowles goes beyond showing us how mid-Victorian ideas about feminism, social class and evolution have affected twentieth-century thought. As he says in 'Notes on an Unfinished Novel', an essay he wrote while *The French Lieutenant's Woman* was still in progress, his purpose is also to make clear that

33

the Victorian Age, especially from 1850 on, was highly existentialist in its personal dilemmas. One can almost invert the reality and say that Camus and Sartre have been trying to lead us, in their fashion, to a Victorian seriousness of purpose and moral sensitivity.[2]

Thus, *The French Lieutenant's Woman* is a historical novel – a novel that seeks to recapture the speech, manners and dress of the period in which it is set – only in part. Fowles makes a genuine effort to be accurate in his portrayal of the people of mid-Victorian England, but is conscious of 'cheating' with the dialogue, because, as he says in 'Notes on an Unfinished Novel', 'the genuine dialogue of 1867 (in so far as it can be heard in books of the time) is far too close to our own to sound convincingly old'. He is therefore obliged to 'pick out the more formal and archaic (even for 1867) elements of spoken speech'[3] for use when he wants to suggest that his characters are being existentially inauthentic – that is, the exponents of conventional mid-Victorian values, and not the uniquely free, self-aware individuals they could become.[4]

Fowles blends aspects of the nineteenth and twentieth centuries in other ways as well. Like Thackeray and other serial novelists, he ends selected chapters on a note of suspense; like Sir Walter Scott and George Eliot (to name only two examples), he prefaces each of his chapters with one or more epigraphs. In addition, he sets *The French Lieutenant's Woman* in Lyme Regis, the setting for Jane Austen's *Persuasion*; bases one of its characters, Sam Farrow, on Sam Weller of Dickens's *Pickwick Papers*; and in an essay entitled 'Hardy and the Hag', acknowledges a large and generalised debt to Hardy.[5]

Throughout, Fowles acts as a traditionally omniscient Victorian narrator, entering the minds of his characters and, on occasion, entering the fiction as a character in his own right. Yet he is careful to emphasise, in the novel's thirteenth chapter, that it is inappropriate for a contemporary novelist to pretend that he is an analogue to God. It is inappropriate because God has become an anachronism in our modern, secular world. The pretence that an author knows everything about the characters he creates must be exposed for what it is, Fowles argues, and the characters themselves must be allowed to behave as though they were free – not as though they were the puppets of an 'omniscient and decreeing' (86) deity.

In Fowles's view, the Victorian novelist/God could create only 'a planned world' (86), a world in which the characters' behaviour is decided in advance, and in which there can be only one outcome.

Fowles is conscious that he cannot altogether avoid fostering the illusion that he himself is an analogue to God; nevertheless, he *can* emphasise that the God to which he corresponds is twentieth century in character, a God definable as 'the freedom that allows other freedoms to exist' (86).[6] Thus Fowles's characters behave not as puppets, but as ostensibly autonomous beings; their lives are shaped not by his overall plan, but by a variety of factors, contingency being foremost amongst them.[7]

The novel's three endings – Chapters 44, 60 and 61 – are the logical outcome of this approach to narration. In the first ending, Charles Smithson abandons his interest in Sarah Woodruff, the intriguing French lieutenant's woman of the title, and returns to his fiancée, the shallow and conventional Ernestina Freeman. Fowles deals perfunctorily with subsequent events: Charles and Ernestina marry and have seven children, Sarah never reappears to trouble Charles again, and various minor characters behave as we might have expected. When in the next chapter we learn that this first ending is one Charles imagined to himself while travelling between London and Exeter, it seems that Fowles included it in the novel to show that his characters are free to behave conventionally if they choose to, but that the conventional endings that result from such behaviour tend to be unsatisfactory.

Why, then, does Fowles present us with a second conventional ending in Chapter 60? Here Charles and Sarah are reunited after a two-year separation, and decide to resume their relationship; it is implicit that they will marry and provide a happy home for Lalage, the child Charles discovers he has fathered. Why Fowles should make the same point about conventionality once again, before describing in the third ending how Charles is reunited with Sarah, but decides to part from her, is not immediately clear.[8]

Charles Scruggs has suggested, interestingly, that the endings provide an opportunity for 'retrospective patterning' – for viewing the complexities in Fowles's presentation of his main characters in three quite different ways.[9] The first conventional ending resolves the complexities in one way, and the second ending in another; the final ending, Chapter 61, is deliberately inconclusive.[10] Scruggs identifies some of the retrospective patterns in *The French Lieutenant's Woman*, but neglects to mention the most important of them all – the novel's tragic patterns, the patterns that suggest it may be in some sense a tragedy. Fowles raises the tragic possibility with us for the sake of asking whether the two main characters act as freely as he has suggested they do, and whether they may be correctly regarded as the novel's hero and heroine.[11]

By the time we reach the novel's first ending in Chapter 44, Sarah, significantly nicknamed 'Tragedy', has twice been involved in a tragic action in the role of heroine. Traditionally, the hero or heroine of a tragedy is someone who is in some sense superior to the members of his or her society, while at the same time being 'neither perfect in virtue and justice, nor one who falls into misfortune through vice and depravity; but rather, one who succumbs through some miscalculation'.[12] If Sarah fulfils the definition of tragic heroine, her first 'miscalculation' occurs when she leaves her position as governess to the Talbot family and follows Varguennes, the French lieutenant of the title, to Exeter. It is odd that she misjudges his character, for if she has a claim to tragic superiority, it surely lies in her skill at '[seeing] through' people:

> [She had] an uncanny... ability to classify other people's worth: to understand them, in the fullest sense of that word. ...She could sense the pretensions of a hollow argument, a false scholarship, a biased logic when she came across them; but she also saw through people in subtler ways. ...[She] saw them as they were and not as they tried to seem. (49–50)

Why Sarah is mistaken about Varguennes may be explained in a number of ways. If she is a tragic heroine, she must be less than 'perfect', but must at the same time stop short of being either vicious or depraved. Her mistake arises from the fact that she is too kind, too trusting and too inexperienced: Fowles points out that, prior to meeting the French lieutenant, Sarah led a sheltered life in which books played a larger part than people. 'Without realising it', he comments, 'she judged people as much by the standards of Walter Scott and Jane Austen as by any empirically arrived at' (50).

In other words, Sarah misjudges Varguennes because she is at first existentially inauthentic: she trusts, mistakenly, not to her own feelings about him, but to the feelings that her reading has engendered within her. In Exeter, however, it becomes clear to her that Varguennes 'was insincere... a liar. ...I saw all this within five minutes of that meeting. ...I tried to see worth in him, respectability, honour. And then I was filled with a kind of rage at being deceived' (151). Here, in tragic terms, Sarah has reached the moment of recognition.

In *Oedipus Rex* that moment comes when the messenger arrives to reveal to Oedipus that he is unwittingly guilty of incest and patricide. Though in many ways an admirable man, Oedipus has made an unintentional mistake, and must suffer for it accordingly. In *Othello* the moment of recognition occurs at the point where Othello recognises the truth about Desdemona. The action of Shakespeare's play arises, of course, from the fact that Othello is flawed by jealousy – for in Renaissance tragedy, it is usually a flaw of character that is responsible for the main character's downfall. Whether, in classical terms, Sarah simply makes a mistake, like Oedipus; or suffers, like a Renaissance protagonist, as a result of 'some deep flaw in my soul [to which] my better self [was] blinded' (150), is not clear.

If Sarah *is* flawed, and her flaw is that she is existentially inauthentic, we may say that her experience with Varguennes gives rise to a new authenticity. She tells Charles that, after returning to Lyme Regis, she saw that if she had continued to work as a governess, she would probably have led no more than a vicariously happy life. It would have been a life spent observing the pleasures of the families she served, while knowing that she herself would 'never have children, a husband, and those innocent happinesses they have' (153).

By leaving her post – by turning her back on Victorian convention and deliberately setting herself apart as the French Lieutenant's Whore – she achieves an existential freedom that the members of the society she spurns simply 'cannot understand' (153). What she experiences is the freedom of living outside mid-Victorian society and the pressure it puts on people to conform to its strictures. But in the absence of a private income, she cannot remain outside her society indefinitely, and rejoins it when a position is found for her in the home of Mrs Poulteney. Fowles has now set the stage for what may be taken to be the novel's second tragic action, with Sarah again serving as heroine, and with the role of antagonist assigned to Mrs Poulteney and all she represents.

In *Othello* the antagonist is Iago, the character who seeks to destroy Othello by casting doubt on Desdemona's fidelity. Where Iago acts purely as an individual driven by 'motiveless malignity', Mrs Poulteney represents the worst excesses of mid-Victorian sanctimoniousness and conventionality. Through her imposition of pious, bourgeois values on the people she employs, she acts as Sarah's antagonist in conjunction with Victorian society as a whole. Though Sarah may be existentially authentic when she enters Mrs Poulteney's household, she is only one person pitted against a formidable collective adversary. As we observe her, we experience the traditional feelings of 'pity and fear' that tragedy arouses – pity for her vulnerability and isolation, and fear for what may happen to her. We can see that, having made one mistake with Varguennes, Sarah may make another with Charles, or may find herself so at odds with Mrs Poulteney – and Victorian society – as to be driven to a tragic end.

The situation is complicated by the fact that Charles, too, conforms to the definition of a tragic protagonist.[13] The son of a baronet, he is superior in social class to most of the other characters in the novel; well-educated and discerning, he is convinced from reading Darwin that he is 'a highly intelligent being, one of the fittest, and endowed with total free will' (164). Yet he is less than perfect: though Fowles emphasises that Charles is neither vicious nor depraved, he feels obliged to point out that his character's 'distinguishing trait' (19) is laziness, and that his 'respect for convention' (29) is often too pronounced. It is significant that, whereas Sarah has a 'tragic face' (13), Charles's face is 'ambiguous' (40), for Fowles deliberately raises our expectations about the latter's tragic status, only to confound them later.

Fowles complicates matters further by hinting in the opening chapters of *The French Lieutenant's Woman* that Sarah may be either the protagonist of a tragic action, or the antagonist whose role it is to bring Charles to a tragic end. Described variously as 'a figure from myth', 'a living memorial to the drowned' (9), and later, as an Odyssean 'siren' or 'Calypso' (125), with 'eyes a man could drown in' (195), Sarah seems a temptress who may lure Charles to his fate. When he first sees her, Charles is struck by her penetrating gaze: '[a]gain and again afterwards', Fowles comments, 'Charles thought of that look as a lance' (13). Here, as elsewhere in the novel, it appears that Sarah's role is to challenge and perhaps ultimately defeat him.[14] Significantly, the fossils that most interest him are 'tests'; when Sarah brings him some particularly good examples of them, we sense that her role in the novel is to test Charles and expose his weaknesses.

If we view Sarah as a destructive temptress, we pity Charles's inability to see her for what she is, and fear that she may bring about his tragic destruction. Our sense that she poses a threat to him is strengthened, moreover, by Fowles's many hints that Charles and his class are in danger from the lower orders. Though he is familiar with Darwin's *The Origin of Species*, he has never heard of Marx, and is therefore unaware that he may be involved in what might be called a

Marxist/Darwinist tragedy.[15] Part of Marx's argument in *Das Kapital* is that as wealth begins to concentrate in the hands of a small minority, the capitalists, that minority will become decadent and weak, and will ultimately be displaced by a stronger and fitter majority. In this context, our feelings of pity and fear for Charles repeatedly come to the fore whenever he shows signs of weakness and decadence. Lazy, wasteful of money, dependent on his servant to do things for him, he clearly belongs to a class of people ill-equipped to survive in the absence of a comfortable income. Fowles hints at a tragic Marxist/Darwinist outcome when he comments that the servant Sam's 'wrong a's and h's were not really comic; they were signs of a social revolution, and this was something Charles failed to recognise' (41). Like Sam, Sarah is a servant (though as a governess, a distinctly superior servant); in the event of revolution, she and the other members of the lower classes, Fowles implies, may bring about Charles's downfall.

Initially Charles interests himself in Sarah's circumstances out of a sense of *noblesse oblige* – a sense that he has a 'certain responsibility towards the less fit' (144) – and also because he is attracted to her in a variety of ways.[16] Once he has confided in Dr Grogan, however, and read the case history of Marie de Morell, the young madwoman who ruined the career of Lieutenant Emile de La Roncière, he begins to regard Sarah as a positive danger not only to his survival but to his freedom. In Chapter 60 Sarah is compared to the Sphinx, and if we are aware of this as we re-read the novel, it may seem that Fowles is preparing us for an ending like that of *Oedipus Rex* – where, many years after answering the riddle of the Sphinx, Oedipus learns that, although he has always believed himself to be free, he has in fact been a pawn of fate.[17]

Despite his ignorance of Marxist doctrine, Charles suspects that not only he but his whole social class is destined for extinction: '...he felt that the enormous apparatus rank required a gentleman to erect around himself was like the massive armour that had been the death warrant of so many ancient saurian species' (253). Immediately prior to the first ending, Charles learns that his inheritance is to be diminished substantially by the unexpected marriage of his uncle. Thus, when he is faced with having to choose between Ernestina and Sarah, the choice that presents itself to him is between his continued survival on the one hand (he sees that he can survive his loss of income by marrying Ernestina and going to work for her father); and on the other, the loss of not only his freedom but perhaps of life itself. It seems to Charles that if he were to choose Sarah, he would become 'one of life's victims, one more ammonite caught in the vast movements of history, stranded now for eternity, a potential turned to a fossil' (289). We might say that this is Charles's moment of tragic recognition, except that it comes *before* he has made his fateful choice.

In Chapter 44, the novel's first ending, Charles chooses Ernestina, and thereby denies us the tragic outcome we have been expecting. Where earlier, his soul was said to be 'one part irony to one part convention' (18), it is clear that the conventional part has triumphed here in the interests of self-preservation. Charles has done his duty, and duty, we are told in the chapter's epigraph, is 'the coward acquiescence/ In a destiny's behest...' (290). With these lines, Fowles intimates that Charles has been cowardly in choosing Ernestina rather than Sarah, and resolves any ambiguities surrounding Charles's status as tragic hero by denying him that status.

Fowles similarly casts doubt on whether Sarah should be viewed as either a tragic antagonist or a tragic heroine. In the light of the novel's first ending, she is clearly not the destructive temptress we might have thought her to be. Instead, she is someone who has made the same mistake twice – that of seeking a new and better life with a man who ultimately declines to marry her. Whatever feelings of pity and fear we may have had are justified by the first ending, where Fowles comments that 'This is what... happens. People sink out of sight, drown in the shadows of closer things' (292).

Ironically, the 'siren' who earlier appeared to be luring Charles to a metaphoric death by drowning suffers that fate herself. Though Fowles is vague about what he means by drowning 'in the shadows of closer things', he seems to be hinting that Sarah has been driven to prostitution.[18] That prospect is clearly in Charles's mind in Chapter 39, when he picks up a prostitute in the murky shadows of a London street, and discovers to his horror that her name, too, is Sarah.[19] Of course the young woman who is seduced and abandoned, then left with no alternative but to sell her body in the streets, is a stock figure in Victorian melodrama, which means that Sarah Woodruff takes on the role in Chapter 44 of Love Betrayed.

Charles and Sarah may be seen to play other roles, though, too, for the first ending admits of many possibilities. Earlier, Dr Grogan has told Charles that Sarah's melancholy is 'a cholera, a typhus of the intellectual faculties. You must think of her like that. Not as some malicious schemer' (194). If we agree with Grogan, we may conclude that in the first ending Charles carefully avoids being 'infected' by her in her role as tragic antagonist; or, taking issue with Grogan, we may argue, as Charles Scruggs does, that Sarah is a latter-day Pamela, and that the reason she never troubles Charles again is that she can see that her plans to trap him into marriage have failed.[20] We cannot, however, say definitively that Sarah is intent on making Charles her husband, because Fowles denies us access to the workings of her mind. Except when she speaks to reveal what she is thinking, Sarah is inscrutable: when she is silent, we can only guess at her motives.[21]

By contrast, Fowles frequently reveals Charles's thoughts. In the chapter immediately following the first ending, he emphasises that what he represented in that ending were the feelings that 'were... present in Charles's own mind. The book of his existence, so it seemed to him, was about to come to a distinctly shabby close' (295). Implicitly, Charles views it as 'shabby' because he has abandoned Sarah with no thought for her future, and because he has made no effort to question his irrational fear that she might contribute to the loss of his freedom. Earlier he agreed with Grogan that 'a human being cannot but see his power of self-analysis as a very special privilege in the struggle to adapt. Both men had seen proof there that man's free will was not in danger' (258). Thus, the novel's first ending represents 'a betrayal of Charles's deeper potentiality' (295), in that his decision to return to Ernestina arises from his failure to subject himself to searching self-scrutiny.

Prior to the first ending there are hints that Charles is an inauthentic character whom Sarah, in the role of Conchis-like mentor, guides towards existential authenticity. In his conversations with her, he sometimes seems 'trite, a mere mouther of convention' (157). Yet, as she tells her story, she clearly has an effect on him: she makes him feel uncomfortably as though he is playing a role rather than living his life as a unique human being. As he listens to her, he feels like a stranger to himself. Eventually he has a glimpse of the 'ideal world' (154) she inhabits, where it is possible for her to experience a 'freedom' that the conventionally bourgeois individual 'cannot understand' (153).

Charles has not achieved existential authenticity by the time he chooses between Sarah and Ernestina, but in the chapter immediately following the first ending, he suddenly realises that he has 'a choice'. 'He had not', Fowles comments, 'the benefit of existentialist terminology; but what he felt was really a very clear case of the anxiety of freedom – that is, the realisation that one *is* free and the realisation that being free is a situation of terror' (296). The fact that he is experiencing this 'anxiety of freedom' means, in existential terms, that he is now at the threshold of authentic self-discovery – the discovery that he is terrifyingly free in a world bereft of God and devoid of moral guidelines.[22]

He now has a choice between continuing to be as he is – a lazy, inauthentic mouther of convention – and seeking to realise his potential as a uniquely authentic individual. Inauthentic existence often manifests itself in the form of the individual's pretending to himself that someone else can take his freedom away. Thus, Charles behaves inauthentically when he chooses Ernestina on the grounds that life with Sarah would necessarily involve the loss of his freedom, but authentically when he later admits to himself that in choosing Sarah, his continued freedom would not be in danger.

Though Charles makes an inauthentic choice in the novel's first ending, he acts authentically a chapter later when he rejects Ernestina in favour of Sarah. Here he discovers, however, that Sarah has earlier lied to him about having slept with Varguennes. 'What duped you was my loneliness', she tells him. 'A resentment, an envy, I don't know.... Do not ask me to explain what I have done. I cannot explain it. It is not to be explained' (308–9). If Sarah dupes Charles in much the same way as Iago dupes Othello, out of 'motiveless malignity' – this being one of the ways in which we might interpret 'It is not to be explained' – Fowles is hinting that at least one of his novel's remaining endings will be tragic.

In Chapter 48 he intrudes into a dialogue between Charles's better and worse selves. 'You know your choice', he says, addressing the former. 'You stay in prison, what your time calls duty, honour, self-respect, and you are comfortably safe. Or you are free and crucified' (314). Adherence to contemporary convention – to notions of duty, honour and self-respect – leads, Fowles is emphasising, to an inauthentic way of life; the alternative, being 'free and crucified', is equivalent to the existential experience of 'the anguish of freedom'. Such anguish arises in the individual who finds the thought of boundless freedom unbearable. Near the conclusion of his inner dialogue, Charles reverses his earlier view of Sarah as a threatening temptress, and, convinced now of her essential goodness, looks upon her as a saviour who might 'uncrucify' him (315). His 'new vision' of unlimited freedom leaves him 'shriven of established religion for the rest of his life', and firm in his belief that Sarah's lies about Varguennes were 'stratagems to unblind him' (318).

In the absence of existentialist terminology, Charles has fashioned for himself what is in effect a religion of freedom. He recognises that he has always been 'an impostor' (330) in his dealings with Ernestina, and begins very tentatively to forge values that are uniquely his own. At first sight it might seem that he is moving closer and closer to becoming existentially authentic. Yet on closer examination it emerges that Charles's formulation of his self-styled religion of freedom is both irrational and cowardly. It is irrational in that Charles makes a Christ-like figure of a woman he had formerly feared was a fatal temptress, and cowardly in that he assumes that freedom is only bearable if there is someone with whom he can share the attendant anxiety. He has yet to acquire the courage to face life's dangers and complexities on his own.

Unsurprisingly, his commitment to his new religion is less than complete. On the one hand he tells Grogan that he was 'perfectly free' (341) when he visited Sarah in Exeter and decided to break off his engagement to Ernestina. In addition, he emphasises that he broke off with her because he wanted to avoid living 'a lifetime of pretence' (340). In writing to Sarah, on the other hand, he speaks inauthentically of the 'strange fate' that brought them together, and adds that, 'God willing, nothing shall take you from me unless it be yourself that wishes it so' (321). God and fate can have no part in the personal philosophy of one who is existentially authentic, for they are the means by which an individual avoids responsibility for his own actions.

In Chapter 58 Fowles comments that 'When [Charles] had had his great vision of himself freed from his age, his ancestry and class and country, he had not realised how much the freedom was embodied in Sarah; in the assumption of a shared exile. He no longer much believed in that freedom; he felt he had merely changed traps, or prisons' (366). Charles now seems to recognise, albeit momentarily, that his religion of freedom is bogus. In the same chapter he distinguishes more clearly than before 'between the real Sarah and the Sarah he had created in so many such dreams: the one Eve personified, all mystery and love and profundity, and the other a half-scheming, half-crazed governess from an obscure seaside town' (367). His association of her with Eve suggests that he fears her – fears that, just as Eve tempted Adam into committing the act that led to their expulsion from the Garden of Eden, so Sarah may lure him to his destruction. Though his trip to America gives Charles 'a kind of faith in freedom' (373), it is a faith rendered tenuous by his anxiety that, once found, Sarah may not be the saviour who guarantees his freedom but rather the temptress who takes it away.

Each of the novel's remaining endings resolves in a different way the uncertainty surrounding the status of the two main characters, as well as Charles's own uncertainty about whether he is free. The first of these, Chapter 60, contains numerous hints to the effect that Charles is a tragic hero, and that ultimately he will find himself in the position of Oedipus at the end of *Oedipus Rex*, aware that, although he has believed himself to be free, he has in fact been subject to forces beyond his control. Thus the chapter begins with Charles's solicitor, Montague, comparing the recently-located Sarah to the Sphinx, and warning him to 'bear in mind what happened to those who failed to solve the enigma' (376). Fowles furthers our expectation of a tragic outcome by commenting that Charles must pass through the 'fatal gate' of the house (377) in which she is now living, and by noting that Sarah's demeanour was 'almost tragic' (389).

In his interview with Sarah, Charles makes use of '[m]elodramatic' language. 'What cried out behind [his words]', though, comments Fowles, 'was not melodrama, but tragedy' (388). Charles finds that Sarah has been living and working in the home of the Rossettis, and that she now gives every appearance of being a 'New Woman' (379), self-supporting and apparently uninterested in marriage. She is an intimidating figure, and causes Charles to reflect that 'Some terrible perversion of human sexual destiny had begun; he was no more than a footsoldier, a pawn in a far vaster battle; and like all battles it was not about love, but about possession and territory' (387). Here Charles appears to experience a moment of tragic self-awareness similar to Oedipus' final awareness that he is a pawn of fate. He sees in Sarah's appearance and independent behaviour evidence that he is part of the process of evolution, and that he is being swept to a tragic end by forces he cannot control.

But, as in the novel's first ending, in Chapter 44, Fowles raises our expectations of a tragic outcome only to disappoint them. In producing Lalage, the child Charles has fathered, Sarah reveals that she has not participated in some 'terrible perversion of human sexual destiny' – has not refused a traditional maternal role – and the chapter ends happily, with a family united. Rather than conclude as a tragedy, as we have been led to expect, Chapter 60 ends as a Providential melodrama, with Charles convinced that the family's reunion 'had been in God's hands, in His forgiveness of their sins' (392–3).[23]

Charles is denied the status of tragic hero in the second ending because it, too, fails to end tragically. Earlier, he has thought of Sarah as a saviour who might 'uncrucify' him (315) – who might relieve him of the existential 'anguish of freedom'. Here he denies his own freedom and assigns responsibility for his reunion with Sarah and Lalage to a benevolent Providence. In existential terms, Charles is behaving inauthentically – he is behaving as though he were subject to the will of God, when in fact (as Fowles has insisted in Chapter 13) he is free. In so doing, Charles denies himself the status of existential hero. Fowles's purpose in having a second conventional ending is now clear: he wants to emphasise that whether Charles chooses Sarah (as in Chapter 60, but not in Chapter 44) is less important than the spirit in which he makes his choice. Authenticity and freedom are the key issues; Sarah is incidental to them.

Though in Chapter 60 Charles regards Sarah as a saviour, she herself is aware of having made some all-too-human mistakes. In the course of their interview, she confesses to him that, in Lyme Regis, 'I... abused your trust, your generosity, I, yes, I [threw] myself at you, forced myself upon you, knowing very well that you had other obligations. ...I believe I was right to destroy what had begun between us. There was a falsehood in it...' (383). It is because she now wishes to behave authentically that she expresses a reluctance to marry Charles – to continue a relationship she believes is founded on 'falsehood'. She makes no reference to Providence, and no effort to pressure Charles into marriage; indeed, she makes a point of retiring from the room to allow him to make his own decision about Lalage and the future of their family – and that is, in existential terms, authentic behaviour. Sarah emerges from the novel's second ending as an existential heroine: it is with this in mind, no doubt, that Fowles refers to her as the novel's 'protagonist' (348) in Chapter 55.

In Chapter 61, the last ending, Charles and Sarah meet as before, though by accident rather than by virtue of Providential design. '[T]here is', says Fowles, 'no intervening god' (398) in this chapter, beyond what can be seen in its first epigraph, an epigraph stating that evolution 'is simply the process by which chance... co-operates with natural law to create living forms better and better adapted to survive' (394). Charles is now convinced of something he only suspects in Chapter 60 – that Sarah is a manipulative schemer who takes pleasure in making 'victim[s]' (388) of the men in her life. Though she refuses to marry him, she hints that she might be willing to continue their relationship as a 'Platonic –

and [eventually]... more intimate, never consecrated – friendship'. Charles sees in this a readiness to 'surrender truth, feeling, perhaps all womanly modesty in order to save her own integrity', and, filled with a sense of his 'own true superiority to her' (397), storms out of her life, coldly refusing to inquire about the small child – presumably Lalage – another occupant of the house is holding in her arms.

If he is right about Sarah's determination to preserve her integrity, she again emerges as an existential heroine, devoted to the concept of authenticity. And although Charles's posturing suggests that he is inauthentic – after leaving her he pictures himself melodramatically as 'the last honourable man on the way to the scaffold' (397)[24] – his decisiveness about no longer needing Sarah to bolster his freedom indicates that he has, as Fowles says,

> at last found an atom of faith in himself, a true uniqueness, on which to build; has already begun... to realise that life, however advantageously Sarah may in some ways seem to fit the role of Sphinx... is not one riddle and [the] failure to guess it,... but is to be, however inadequately, emptily, hopelessly into the city's iron heart, endured. And out again, upon the unplumb'd, salt, estranging sea. (399)

The last sentence in this passage, the last in the novel, echoes a line from Matthew Arnold's 'To Marguerite' (1853), a poem Charles has 'committed to heart' (365), and raises problems with respect to Charles's attitude to freedom and to the existential authenticity of the Chapter 61 ending. Arnold's poem tells how the ancient continents were joined together, only to be divided by the seas, and suggests that people are like those continents, wanting to be reunited in love. Clearly, Charles has memorised this poem because, prior to Chapter 61, he has yearned to resume his romantic involvement with Sarah. In the last stanza, quoted in Chapter 58 of the novel, Arnold asks:

> Who order'd, that their longing's fire
> Should be, as soon as kindled, cool'd?
> Who renders vain their deep desire? –
> A God, a God their severance ruled;
> And bade betwixt their shores to be
> The unplumb'd, salt, estranging sea. (366)

Fowles's use of the last line of this poem in the concluding sentence of his novel might suggest that he intends Chapter 61 to be a conventionally tragic ending, with God intervening malevolently at the last moment to separate Charles and Sarah. That, however, would be inconsistent with his attitude to freedom earlier in the novel, and with his stated intention, in Chapter 55, to present two quite different endings. What seems more probable is that Fowles echoes the line from Arnold for the sake of suggesting that however hard he has tried to make his characters seem free, as their author he is ultimately the God who separates them.

He separates them in Chapter 61 for the sake of emphasising that true freedom is only to be found in solitude (not in the company of a saviour figure) on the 'unplumb'd sea' of life – the sea representing life's unfathomed depths, its flux and hidden complexities. Charles may perish tragically on the voyage, but Fowles 'think[s] not': having acquired a certain 'faith in himself' (399), it is more probable that he will ultimately become existentially authentic. This would be consistent with the kind of 'retrospective patterning' that takes into account Charles's early enthusiasm for freedom and his dawning awareness that 'life, however advantageously Sarah may in some ways seem to fit the role of Sphinx... is not one riddle and [the] failure to guess it' (399). Because that awareness is denied him earlier, it is not available for inclusion in the patterns we form when we read the first and second endings. The third ending implies, as the others do not, that Charles may ultimately escape his Victorian 'prison' (314) – duty, honour and conventionality – and, that after much soul-searching, may finally attain to existential authenticity.

5

The Ebony Tower

Inspiration to write *The Ebony Tower* stories came to Fowles suddenly, and he interrupted work on both *Daniel Martin* and his revision of *The Magus* to give them his full attention.[1] In a note to the second story, 'Eliduc' (actually a translation of a twelfth-century tale by Marie de France), he says that the 'working title of this collection of stories was *Variations*, by which I meant to suggest variations both on certain themes in previous books of mine and in methods of narrative presentation...' (117). Later, however, in an interview with John Baker, he emphasised that the stories struck him as being variations on his earlier fictions only *after* he had written them, and spoke of being 'amused by the detective work some critics have put in trying to find the links between them'.[2] 'It wasn't until I'd finished the title story', he added, 'that I was struck by the echoes of the old French tale of Eliduc, and I wrote that in, and the incident of killing the weasel on the road, afterward.'[3]

Thus, although we may find parallels between Fowles's earlier fiction and the five stories in *The Ebony Tower*, or even between the stories themselves, the parallels are in general less important than the complexities of each story taken by itself. Significantly, *The Ebony Tower* contains the first signs of Fowles's waning interest in existentialism, as though in anticipation of some statements he was to make only a few years after the collection was published. 'I now think of existentialism as a kind of literary metaphor, a wish fulfilment', he told Christopher Bigsby in 1982. 'I long ago began to doubt whether it had any true philosophical value in many of its assertions about freedom.'[4] To Susana Onega, seven years later, he added, 'I... am [no] longer an existentialist in [either] the social sense, [or] the cultural sense... I am really much more interested, in terms of the modern novel, in what fiction is about.'⁵ Yet in 1988 he told Katherine Tarbox that 'Mystery... lies in things and in gaps in the story... I regard all that in books as symbolic of the general mystery in cosmic, existential terms.'⁶ Though doubtful about existentialism – doubtful enough for his interest in 'what fiction is about' to have displaced his early interest in existential freedom – Fowles nevertheless continued, in the eighties, to accept the existential view that the world is endlessly complex and mysterious. He continued, too, to believe that its 'general mystery' should be symbolised in the complexity of contemporary fiction.

While the later stories in *The Ebony Tower* focus both on the nature of fiction and the complexity of the world at large, the title story is concerned with one of the problems that existentialism raises but fails to solve. Near the end, the main character, David Williams, is presented with a dilemma similar to the one Charles Smithson faces in *The French Lieutenant's Woman*.⁷ In the last two chapters of that novel, Charles must choose between marrying Sarah on the one hand, and venturing alone upon the uncharted 'sea of life' on the other. If the narrator of *The French Lieutenant's Woman* knew everything about his characters' past, present and future, he could tell us which is the better choice of the two. But in Chapter 13 Fowles makes a point of stressing that the narrator's omniscience is spurious, and leaves us to decide for ourselves what Charles should do. Our choice is not guided by a truly omniscient narrator, but it is guided, nevertheless: Fowles's high regard for existential authenticity is evident in many of the earlier chapters of *The French Lieutenant's Woman*, and has a powerful influence on our sense that the final, existential chapter is the one in which Charles makes the choice that is more personally fulfilling.

At the end of 'The Ebony Tower', by contrast, the question of whether the main character should leave his family in the interests of becoming authentic is left both unanswered and unguided. As we have seen, Fowles altered the ending of the story to include a variation on an incident in the twelfth-century tale, 'Eliduc', by Marie de France. Here a character named Guildelüec observes a weasel restore its mate to life by placing a red flower in its mouth, and succeeds in bringing her husband's mistress back from the dead by quick-wittedly placing the same flower in the mistress's mouth. In Fowles's counterpart to this incident in 'The Ebony Tower', the main character, David Williams, accidentally runs over a weasel as he drives to Paris, and stops his car to investigate. 'It was dead, crushed. Only the head had escaped. A tiny malevolent eye still stared up, and a trickle of blood, like a red flower, had spilt from the gaping mouth' (107).

It might seem that Fowles's purpose here is to emphasise that the supernatural is all very well in twelfth-century romance, but that it has no place in contemporary literature. The supernatural has an important part to play in 'The Ebony Tower', however, for during his visit to the French country home of an elderly British painter, Henry Breasley, Williams finds himself falling increasingly under the 'spell' (97) not only of the house and its grounds, but of Diana, a young woman who is staying with Breasley. Diana (nicknamed 'The Mouse', a variation, as Breasley says, on 'The Muse'), admires Williams's work, and confides to him that although Breasley would like to marry her, she would prefer the story of her life to have a 'fairy-tale' (98) ending, in which she, a 'sleeping princess' (98), were rescued by a handsome young prince. Williams, of course, is the prince she has in mind.

Though flattered, Williams is aware that the life he has led prior to meeting Diana has been less than princely: dismayingly, it has been that of a man who is existentially inauthentic. Picturing himself as 'a being bereft of freedom whose true nature he had only just seen' (102), he toys with the idea of joining her in France so that she might lead him, as Sarah Woodruff leads Charles, towards greater authenticity and freedom. But this would mean that Williams would have to leave his wife and children, and despite the fact that choosing not to means living the life of 'an artificial man' (108), or of a caged monkey 'allowed a [single] glimpse of his lost true self' (109), he returns to his family. In doing so, he misses the 'existential chance' (109) – significantly, this is the only place in *The Ebony Tower* in which the term 'existential' is used – of achieving authenticity by leaving his family to start a new life with Diana.

Breasley, an artist who has spent his life spurning bourgeois convention, is an example of the kind of painter Williams might have become – a painter who has developed his talent to the full by dedicating himself exclusively to art. Williams would also like to realise his potential as an artist, and in the process attain to existential authenticity; however, his commitment to his family is too great to make this possible. If he had chosen Diana, Fowles told an interviewer in 1981, Williams 'might have become a better artist, but he would have betrayed his moral being. I'm pointing out that being an artist is an appallingly selfish business; the story is really about the problems, the agonies of being an artist.'[8]

The problems of being an artist in this story are inextricably bound up with the problems of being an existentialist, for to become authentic, the artist must live his life as independently of other people as possible. In Breasley's case, this means becoming excruciatingly lonely in old age, while for Williams it would mean abandoning his family, and thereby breaking the commandment that is impressed on Nicholas Urfe in *The Magus*: 'Thou shalt not inflict unnecessary pain'. Though Fowles extols the virtues of existentialism in his earlier fictions, in 'The Ebony Tower' he suggests that existentialism fails to deal satisfactorily with the question of how to choose between the individual's need to become more authentic on the one hand, and his or her responsibility to family and friends on the other.

Since 'The Ebony Tower' is closely related to 'Eliduc', we might have expected to learn from Fowles's preface to the latter that Marie de France's characters are existentialists before their time – just as, in *The French Lieutenant's Woman*, Fowles says frankly of Charles that while he did not have 'the benefit of existentialist terminology', he nevertheless experienced 'a very clear case of the anxiety of freedom' (296). No such statement is, however, made about Eliduc or any of the other characters in Marie de France's story. Fowles comes closest to claiming that there is an existentialist element in it near the end of his preface, where he says that Marie 'did for her posterity something of what Jane Austen did for hers – that is, she set a new standard for accuracy over human emotions and their absurdities' (120). This comment echoes one that Fowles made to Roy Newquist in 1964, quoted in the Introduction, to the effect that Jane Austen was a 'very existentialist novelist... Most of the time she was writing about a moral tradition, attempting to establish what authenticity was in her particular world and circumstances'.[9]

Fowles's praise both for the 'accuracy over human emotions and their absurdities' in 'Eliduc', and for Jane Austen's presentation of existentially 'authentic' characters in her novels might suggest that the twelfth-century tale is in his view a precursor of the existential novel. However, as the story itself makes clear, that claim cannot be sustained. The crux of the tale comes when Eliduc's wife, Guildelüec, saves the life of Guilliadun, his mistress. Had she not intervened to help Guilliadun, Guildelüec might have retained both her husband and her place at court. But with Guilliadun alive and a rival for her husband's affections, Guildelüec is faced with a choice: whether to try to win her husband back, or instead, to acknowledge that Eliduc has ceased to love her, to start a new life without him. In deciding to accept not only that her marriage is over, but that it would be best for her to enter a nunnery, Guildelüec does *not* act existentially, for what she is doing is trading her adherence to one social institution, marriage, for another – the Catholic Church. Since it would be much easier for her to assume the role of cast-off wife, a figure who, though pitied, would probably still have wealth and influence at court, her decision is authentic in the sense that it is based on what she really feels – that life at court as Eliduc's ex-wife would be impossibly humiliating – rather than on what, by convention, she *ought* to feel (the outrage of a woman betrayed). But it is not an *existential* decision, for it is not made in the belief that the world is completely without moral guidelines, or that the individual who is true to him- or herself must make choices without reference to, or reliance on, established institutions and values. Guildelüec's decision is between one human institution and another: to argue that entering a nunnery is an existential act would be to enlarge the definition of the term 'existential' to a point where it would cease to be meaningful.

In the collection's third story, 'Poor Koko', the question of existential authenticity plays a part, but a smaller part than the question of 'what fiction is about'. The story's nameless first-person narrator, an elderly man of letters, focuses on the problems that a first-person narrator (and, by extension, each of us) must face in trying to arrive at the truth about past experience. The task he has set himself is that of recounting as truthfully as he can the events of the night he was surprised by a burglar while staying in a country cottage owned by friends.

At the time the encounter took place, says the narrator, he could see that he had 'the makings of a story to dine out on for months to come' (158). A professional writer, he has all the skills needed to construct an entertaining account of what passed between the intruder and himself. He even has 'a small skill at mimicking accents' (162), and could use it for comic effect in recalling what the young man said to him. When he comes to write his account, however, he takes great care to avoid misrepresenting what was said and done. Though the terms 'thriller', 'tragedy' and 'melodramatic' (145) appear on the first page of his story, the narrator is at pains not to distort his experiences in order to satisfy the conventions of an established literary form. 'If books have not taught me to admire and desire truth in writing', he says, 'I have wasted my entire life, and the last thing I wish to do in this account is to present myself as other than I am' (146).

Books have played an important part in his life-long search for truth. Yet there are numerous barriers to discovering the truth that are an inescapable part of writing, only some of which the narrator recognises.[10] One such barrier is that writers cannot enter the minds of other people to discover what they are thinking. The best they can do is to infer the thoughts of other people from listening to what they say, observing what they do, and being alert to how other people behave towards them. When the intruder decides to burn the materials that the narrator of 'Poor Koko' has gathered for a critical biography of Peacock, the young man says nothing about how he arrived at his decision, which means that the narrator can only guess at his motives – and this, of course, is the crux of the story.

Writers who seek to represent what other people are thinking are necessarily writers of fiction, for everything they say about the thoughts of others can only be speculative. This is the first barrier to discovering the truth about the past, and an important aspect of 'what fiction is about'. The second barrier is that writers may colour, or even badly distort, their actions (including the act of writing), by making use of coloured or distorted experiences from the past. Thus, when the narrator tells us that 'books – writing them, reading, reviewing, helping to get them into print – have been my life rather more than life itself' (147), we are reminded that Sarah's inauthentic behaviour at the beginning of *The French Lieutenant's Woman*, which arises from her habit of trusting not to her own feelings, but to the feelings that her reading of Jane Austen and Sir Walter Scott has created within her. Significantly, the narrator of 'Poor Koko' tells us that he prefers 'nature in art to nature in actuality' (148), and admits that his major work to date, *The Dwarf in Literature*, is not 'quite the model of objective and erudite analysis it pretended to be' (147) – for he himself is shorter than average, and seems to have written the book in part, at least, in compensation for this.

Between first hearing the burglar rummaging around downstairs and actually meeting him, he has time to speculate on what the intruder is like, and we are not surprised to find that the picture he forms of him is inaccurate. Though the narrator initially imagines him to be a 'long-haired village lout, with fists like hams and a mind to match' (150), a product of 'all the fictional horrors... I had ever seen or read of' (155), he has been deceived by his reading, for the burglar is in fact very different. From speaking to him, the narrator is surprised to find, for example, that the young man is reasonably well-read, is intelligent enough to be selective about what he takes from the houses he burgles, and is kind-hearted enough to treat an older man gently and with consideration. Clearly, his first image of the burglar is a fictional one, for it is coloured by not first- but second-hand knowledge of the world – the knowledge that derives from his reading. Here again we see an aspect of 'what fiction is about'.

In retrospect, the narrator recognises that his own life has been narrow, and that the young man has brought him into contact with a world of which he has no first-hand experience. Not only is it a world of crime; it is a world in which Marxist doctrine is all but religion, and can be quoted as a justification for theft. Thus, the narrator is made to feel that having a comfortable flat in London is a sin against the unspoken commandment that 'thou shalt not own more than a grubby backstreet pad' (157). In the burglar's view, the only real criminals are the rich: '...my house', he says, 'has had burglars in since the day I was born... You know what Marx said? The poor can't steal from the rich. The rich can only rob the poor' (157).

Opposed to the burglar's near-religion of Marxism is the narrator's devotion to 'Humanism, [g]ood manners' and 'common... decency' (161). 'I would give a great deal – I think even an absolution', he says, '...to know when [the burglar made his decision to burn the Peacock materials]' (178). Here the same narrator who is unable to enter the mind of the burglar arrogantly implies that he has the powers of a priest to absolve the young man of the sins he has committed against humanist values. Near the end of the story, however, he admits to feeling guilty himself: 'I *was*', he says, 'guilty of a deafness' (183).

What he means by this is evident from some of the judgemental statements he makes about the burglar early in the story. He deplores the fact, for example, that the young man has no apparent respect for 'language and intellectual honesty', because he and others of his generation 'mistakenly believe them to be shamefully bourgeois' (157); elsewhere, he says condescendingly that he would like to make the burglar 'a shade more aware of the complexities of life' (162). Yet when the young man suggests that the narrator write about the younger generation, the latter protests: 'I couldn't write about something I don't begin to understand' (169). The narrator is 'deaf' to what the burglar has been trying to tell him about himself, because at the time of the burglary, he has no wish to know about it.

In writing about it later, however, he must consider the burglar's point of view if he is to discover why the young man chose to burn his research materials. He entertains a number of possibilities, ultimately rejecting all but one. 'My sin', he says, 'was not primarily that I was middle-class, intellectual, that I may have appeared more comfortably off financially than I am in fact; but that I live by words' (182), whose 'magic power' (183) he has failed to confer on the young burglar. Were the young man more articulate, and less dependent on slang and political catchphrases, he would, the narrator implies, be in a much better position to make an honest living and develop an appreciation of life's complexities.

The narrator's failure to hand on the 'magic' of language is presented partly as one generation's failure to serve the next. The 'Poor Koko' of the title refers, the narrator tells us, to the Japanese concept of 'correct filial behaviour, the proper attitude of son to father' – though he adds that 'I shouldn't like to see it attached to only one of the two' (184). By this he means not only that the burglar's attitude to him, as a member of the older generation, is disrespectful, but that his own attitude to the burglar is lacking in concern for the welfare of the inarticulate young. The story's epigraph, from Old Cornish ('Too long a tongue, too short a hand;/ But tongueless man has lost his land' [184]) similarly suggests that the man who lacks the 'magic power' of language – the 'tongueless man' – will be dispossessed of his birthright; and that if too much of an educated man's life is spent in the world of books, rather than in the everyday world, he will lose touch with a basic obligation to others – the obligation to nurture in them a love of language. Though it has always been open to the narrator, as an articulate member of the middle class, to assist the inarticulate to acquire the 'magic power' of language, this is something he has failed to do.

At first sight, 'Poor Koko' might seem to be yet another fiction in which a Fowles character – in this case the story's narrator – acquires greater existential authenticity. The question of authenticity is, however, more problematic here than in his earlier fiction. For although it may seem from the narrator's admission, early in the story, that 'books... have been my life rather more than life itself' (147), that he is as inauthentic as Sarah at the beginning of *The French Lieutenant's*

Woman, by the time we reach the end of the story, it is not clear that he has made much progress towards authenticity. When he says that his book, *The Dwarf in Literature*, is not as objective as it might have been, indicating that he is now more authentic than when he wrote it, we are unable to evaluate this statement, since Fowles neither presents us with excerpts from the book, nor flashes back in time to show us what the narrator was like when he wrote it. Similarly, although the narrator returns to his Peacock biography with a changed attitude and renewed vigour, we have no evidence that the biography is necessarily better – that is, written by a more authentic author – than it would otherwise have been, since Fowles does not allow us to compare the two versions of it. This is in direct contrast to, say, *The Collector*, where the differences between Miranda's early, inauthentic diary entries and her later ones, written after she has shed the influence of her school and family, are readily apparent.

Nor is it altogether clear that the narrator of 'Poor Koko' has hit on the right explanation for the intruder's behaviour. Towards the end of the story, he confesses that he 'cannot be sure that [he has] reproduced the events of the night with total accuracy' (177); he has tried, but if some sort of bias – whether conscious or unconscious – has coloured his narrative, he may be mistaken about the burglar's intentions. The young man may have burned his research materials as a protest against the narrator's failure to pass on the 'magic' of language; but it is also possible that his behaviour was motivated by resentment of the narrator's life of ease, an aspect of which he wished to spoil. In other words, it may be that the narrator is so self-deceived that complete existential authenticity will continue to elude him as long as he continues to live the precious life of a man of letters.

Other explanations for the burglar's behaviour also offer themselves, for the ever-elusive key to 'Poor Koko' is what was going on in the burglar's mind when he decided to reduce the narrator's papers to so much 'cremated human knowledge' (173). Lacking the omniscience of God, the narrator can only speculate on the young man's motives; as readers, we simply have no way of evaluating how valid his speculations are. Nor are we able to evaluate how much more authentic the narrator is at the conclusion to the story, for it is not altogether clear how inauthentic he was at the beginning. More generally, Fowles is questioning whether existential authenticity is achievable, for the barriers to writing accurately about the past in this story, and thereby gaining greater self-knowledge, are clearly evident to the reader.

As in 'Poor Koko', so in 'The Enigma', the reader is invited to play the role of detective in the interests of solving a mystery. But whereas in the former story the mystery consists in why a young burglar decided to burn the narrator's research materials, in 'The Enigma' it is a matter of explaining the sudden disappearance of Marcus Fielding, a prosperous lawyer, landowner and Member of Parliament. Fowles presents us with various lines of speculation as to what happened to Fielding the afternoon he disappeared, but invites us to pay special attention to the theory of Isobel Dodgson, a would-be writer of fiction, and the girlfriend of Fielding's son.

It is no accident that Ms Dodgson's surname links her to Charles Dodgson, better known as Lewis Carroll, for 'The Enigma' poses a puzzle as ultimately unanswerable as Carroll's famous riddle, 'Why is a raven like a writing-desk?'[11] The mystery of Fielding's disappearance is not, however, simply a puzzle for its own sake, but is one that bears on the larger question of 'what fiction is about'. At first it might seem that Fowles is inviting us to consider the more specialised question of what *detective* fiction is about. But 'The Enigma' is not strictly speaking a detective story, for the mystery it invites us to consider is never finally solved. 'I don't... care a damn for pat endings', Fowles told Robert Robinson in an interview in 1974. 'I think they are absolutely necessary in the strict detective genre, but I am not in that business.'[12] Nor is Fowles in the business of writing exclusively about existential authenticity or freedom, either in this story or any of the others in *The Ebony Tower*. His real interest is in the nature of fiction and the 'general mystery' posed by the world at large – a mystery too complex to yield to a definitive explanation.

Mike Jennings, the detective assigned to the case after preliminary investigation has failed to discover what happened to Fielding, begins by listing twenty possible explanations for his disappearance. As he interviews the people who were closest to Fielding, he begins to see that none of them knew him very well, and that none has an explanation that will do. He rejects suicide, murder, abduction, and so on, as possibilities, and has begun to feel that there is no solution to the mystery at all, when he meets Isobel Dodgson. Unlike the other people who knew Fielding, Isobel has the mind of a novelist, and although she does not make use of existential terminology, suggests to Jennings that the missing man was hopelessly inauthentic. Isobel asks him to view Fielding as though he were a character in fiction, created not by an author, but by a system that demanded he play a role, or rather, a series of roles, that ensured his inauthenticity. Obliged to act the parts of lawyer, Conservative MP, landowner and so on, Fielding, she theorises, decided to walk out on a hollow life. She believes that he committed suicide, and that his body is to be found at the bottom of a lake on the grounds of his country estate.

Most critics find Isobel's theory perfectly acceptable, not least because it is consistent with Fowles's earlier fiction, in which existential theory plays an important part. As if to encourage an existential interpretation of the story, Fowles hints that, like Sarah in *The French Lieutenant's Woman*, Isobel may have the power to help other people attain to authenticity. 'Something about her', he comments, entering Jennings' mind, 'possessed something that he lacked: a potential that lay like unsown ground, waiting for just this unlikely corn-goddess; a direction he could follow, if she would only show it' (228–9). Yet Jennings may be deceived about this, just as (in his superiors' opinion) he is deceived about the validity of Isobel's theory. When he offers it to them as an explanation for Fielding's disappearance, his request to have the lake behind Tetbury Hall dragged is denied, and he is told 'to go away and get on with the job of digging up some hard evidence instead of wasting his time on half-baked psychology' (239).

The problem with Isobel's explanation, of course, is the one we examined in 'Poor Koko'. Just as the narrator of that story is unable to enter the mind of the burglar, so Isobel is unable to gain access to Fielding's innermost thoughts, because, unless he spoke to her confessionally during the crucial two hours she refuses to discuss with Jennings, he has concealed them from her. But even if Fielding *did* speak to her, there is no evidence that he necessarily told her the truth about his situation. Various characters have told Jennings that Fielding worked too hard as a solicitor, Member of Parliament and gentleman farmer. He may have decided to leave the world of getting and spending to join a monastery, as his daughters suspect. If he spoke to Isobel, his story may have been a fiction designed to throw her, and others like her, off his trail. In any case, Isobel cannot claim to *know* what happened to Fielding because, unlike the narrator of the story, she is an ostensible human being, not an omnisicient analogue to God. Her existential explanation of Fielding's disappearance is only one of a number of possible explanations, which is why Fielding's disappearance remains an 'enigma'.

The real mystery in this story, however, is not that of Fielding's disappearance, a mystery that arises from various gaps in what we are able to learn about his final hours. The real mystery is instead the 'general mystery in cosmic... terms' that the story of Fielding parallels. Just as no one can explain his disappearance satisfactorily, so no one can say definitively that he or she knows everything there is to know about either the microcosm (the individual human being) or the macrocosm (the world at large). In his epigraph to 'The Enigma', Fowles poses a question first raised by Tao Te Ching: 'Who can become muddy and yet, settling, slowly become limpid?' (185). That question is answered by 'Marcus Fielding' if we accept Isobel's explanation for his disappearance, but by silence if we recognise that Fowles's overall point is that no one is 'limpid'. We can know nothing with absolute certainty – including whether twentieth-century existentialism is the best of all possible philosophies – because, unlike the omniscient author, who by convention knows everything about the characters he creates, none of us knows everything there is to know about ourselves, other people, or the world as a whole.

'The Cloud' similarly comments on 'the general mystery' and on 'what fiction is about' in its presentation of the uncertainty that characterises life in the twentieth century. Here, as in 'The Enigma', an omniscient narrator tells the story, though in the present tense, rather than the past, suggesting that the characters' future is something that he has not yet witnessed, and is therefore unable to reveal to us. Omniscient about the here and now, however, he is able to enter the minds of two of the characters – Catherine, whose husband has evidently committed suicide, and Peter, a television producer with whom, near the end of the story, she has sexual relations.

Catherine appears to be existentially inauthentic when called upon to tell her young niece, Emma, a story, for the fairy tale she tells – a tale of her own devising – is one in which a princess meets a handsome prince and lives happily ever after. In context, it is clear that the story is a wish-fulfilment for Catherine, who, in her grief for her husband, is yearning for a factitious solution to her problems (the arrival of a Prince Charming), rather than trying to solve them herself, as someone who is existentially authentic would.

Just as Catherine wants to play the role of the princess in her story, so we see in Sally, another of the characters, someone who is playing the role of 'trendy girl-friend' (247), and in Peter, someone who plays a number of selfish, inconsiderate roles in succession. 'One didn't really care what people thought', Peter reflects to himself at one point, 'cutting through other people's crap was what one was about; getting things done, flannelling here, riding roughshod there; have the game played by one's own quick rules' (286). Like Nicholas Urfe at the beginning of *The Magus*, Peter is an inauthentic man who uses people for his own ends – and so is his girlfriend, Sally, though she is less cynical in outlook.

But if this is a story about existential authenticity (and there are good reasons to believe it is not), it shows us no more about Peter and Sally than that they are *irremediably* inauthentic, like Clegg in *The Collector*. Similarly, it reveals no more about Paul and Annabel, than that, as apparently authentic characters – Catherine considers them to be 'real' (248) – they are concerned for her welfare. Nor is there any firm evidence that Catherine herself becomes more authentic in the course of the story, since it is not clear at the end whether she chooses to stay behind in the woods after the picnic to commit suicide or think her way through to greater authenticity. If 'The Cloud' is meant to extol the virtues of existential authenticity, as *The Collector*, *The Magus* and *The French Lieutenant's Woman* are, it fails in its purpose. For it records neither a movement from inauthenticity to authenticity in the case of Catherine, Sally and Paul, nor a movement from authenticity to greater authenticity in the case of Paul and Annabel. As an account of growing existential awareness, it is unsatisfactorily static.

Significantly, Fowles places Roland Barthes' *Mythologies* at the centre of the story, rather than any existential text. Without mentioning the essay by name, Catherine points out that in 'The Blue Guide', Barthes says of tourist guides that they pander to the bourgeois view that 'all utilitarian and all modern things are monotonous. The only interesting things are ancient monuments and the picturesque' (267).[13] This is of interest to Peter, who is a television producer, and can see the potential for a programme on Barthes. Of greater interest to Catherine, however, is the way in which Barthes makes people 'aware of how they communicate and try to control one another. The relation between the overt signs, whether they're verbal or not, and the real meaning of what is happening' (270). Signifi-

cantly, the story's epigraph, 'O, you must wear your rue with a difference' (243), from *Hamlet*, is part of a speech in which Ophelia signals
not only that she is grieving for her father, Polonius, but that her
grief has driven her mad.[14]

Catherine, too, wears her 'rue with a difference', in that she thinks,
less than rationally, that her own 'sign' is

> alpha, one is precious (oh, yes), rare, one sees. One has committed a
> terrible crime, which proves one sees, since no one else admits its
> existence. One sawed the branch one was sitting on. One fouled
> one's own nest. (287)

The 'terrible crime' she fears she has committed – the crime no one else
will acknowledge, since it may have arisen from selfishly making herself
alpha (putting herself first in her marriage), and undermining her
husband's will to live (metaphorically sawing 'the branch one was sitting
on', or fouling 'one's own nest') – is that of having driven him, ultimately, to suicide. Racked by guilt, and in her grief and confusion
'erotic and self-defiled' (287), Catherine sends mixed signals to Peter.
When he comes upon her sunbathing by herself in the forest, she
simply stares at him through her dark glasses at first, apparently willing
him to go away. But when he turns to leave, her 'fingers catch him just
above the bare ankle, the briefest clutch, but enough to stop him' (289).
The fingers signal that she wants him to smooth some sun tan lotion on
her back, and later, that she would have no objection if he were to have
sex with her. But it clearly *is* a matter of having sex rather than making
love, for Catherine is a passive, barely co-operative partner. Earlier in
the story, she has described Peter to herself as 'a worthless, shallow little
prick' (266): whatever her need for sex is prompted by, it is clearly not
respect or affection.

We might assume that Catherine's seduction of Peter is an irrational
act of loneliness; however, Fowles has said that it came to him initially
as the product of 'exorcising self-disgust'.[15] In other words, sex with a
man she despises appears to be a self-imposed penance for the 'crime'
of causing her husband to kill himself. Whether or not she is guilty of
this crime is impossible to say, since none of the other characters makes
any reference to it, and the omniscient narrator, though capable of
telling us, maintains a discreet silence. Nor is it possible for us to judge
whether the penance is sufficient to exorcise her feelings of guilt. Her

disappearance at the end of the story, just as a dark cloud looms to spoil an otherwise perfect day, may suggest that she found her experience with Peter degrading rather than cleansing. If at the end she has chosen to commit suicide, it would appear that she has been driven to it by guilt over the part she may have played in her husband's death, and by shame over her seduction of Peter.

Earlier in the story, the possibility of suicide is hinted at when she asks Paul, 'Are you and Bel frightened I shall try to kill myself as well?' (260). A further hint is to be found in Fowles's preface to 'Eliduc', where he speaks of having 'a dead weasel on my conscience; and deeper still, a dead woman' (117), for Catherine is the only woman in the collection to either die or be threatened by imminent death. Yet it is not entirely clear that she takes her own life at the end of 'The Cloud', for in the fairy tale she tells her niece, the princess spends a long time wandering in the woods before finally being reunited with her prince – and it may be that Catherine has chosen to withdraw from the group in the confused hope of miraculously meeting the man who can solve all her problems.

Interestingly, Fowles has commented that he did not mean to suggest that Catherine necessarily commits suicide.[16] A further possibility is that she may simply be retiring from the group to give herself time to think. It would be inconsistent with Catherine's state of confusion, and with Fowles's theme of the impossibility of knowing anything with certainty, if the dark cloud at the end were to be any but an ambiguous sign. Its appearance at the end of the story may suggest Catherine has reached a black period in her life that must end in suicide; or alternatively, that although she must suffer for a short period of time before the sun metaphorically returns, she will eventually begin to enjoy life again. Other interpretations are also possible, depending on what we make of the cloud's relationship to Catherine's situation. However, no single interpretation will do, for like the ending of 'The Enigma', where we remain uncertain as to what happened to the missing Fielding, the ending of 'The Cloud' serves as a counterpart to the inscrutable 'general mystery' posed by the world at large.

The Ebony Tower represents a watershed in Fowles's development as a writer. Whereas his earlier works of fiction – *The Collector*, *The Magus* and *The French Lieutenant's Woman* – extol the virtues of existentialism, the stories in this collection are expressive of his growing scepticism about it. The title story draws into question the main character's need to choose between living an existentially authentic life on the one hand, and remaining with his wife and family on the other. While in Fowles's earlier fictions the former alternative is made to seem attractive, in 'The Ebony Tower', choosing to become authentic is presented as being self-indulgent and irresponsible, for Fowles also sees the need for the individual to honour his family obligations.

In the remaining stories, existentialism is only tangential to Fowles's main concerns. 'Eliduc' presents one of its characters, Guildelüec, with a choice, but rather than being an existential choice, it is one between two human institutions – marriage and the Church. Similarly, 'Poor Koko' and 'The Enigma' dwell not on specifically existential matters, but on generalised questions about the limits of human knowledge – and 'The Cloud' is clearly just as concerned with Roland Barthes' theory of signs as with existential theory. As in 'The Cloud', so even more clearly in his next novel, *Daniel Martin*, Fowles reveals his doubts about the 'true philosophical value' of existentialism, and largely abandons his early fascination with that philosophy to explore new and different areas of interest.[17]

6

Daniel Martin

Daniel Martin arose, as *The French Lieutenant's Woman* did, from an image that came spontaneously to Fowles's mind. 'It was of a woman', he told Susana Onega, 'standing in a desert somewhere. I did not at that time even know where it was. She seemed to be weeping, to be lost, a moment of total desolation.'[1] While this image of a single, suffering woman in desolate surroundings might suggest that Fowles's novel portrays an individual in an existential world bereft of moral and spiritual guidelines, *Daniel Martin* is not in any straightforward sense an existential novel. As in *The Ebony Tower*, which he interrupted *Daniel Martin* to write, Fowles brings certain aspects of existentialism into question, though less radically than in the stories.[2] Rather than question existential theory in *Daniel Martin*, Fowles merely observes that existentialism, though important in the 1950s and 1960s, has by the mid-1970s had its day. Such is his lingering fascination, however, with the philosophy, that he dwells on two key existential questions in the novel: 'What are some of the barriers to attaining a sense of personal authenticity?' and 'Can these barriers be surmounted?'

Daniel Martin opens with the statement, 'Whole sight; or all the rest is desolation', echoing a line in Matthew Arnold's famous poem, 'To a Friend', in which the poet offers his thanks to Sophocles,

> ...whose even-balanced soul,
> From first youth tested up to extreme old age,
> Business could not make dull, nor passion wild;
> Who saw life steadily, and saw it whole;
> The mellow glory of the Attic stage,
> Singer of sweet Colonus, and its child.[3]

The individual who sees life steadily and sees it whole, Fowles suggests in *Daniel Martin*, is the one who has a clear sense of his own authenticity, a concept that must not be associated exclusively with the existentialists.[4] Fowles wants to claim that Matthew Arnold (like Charles Smithson) is an existentialist before his time, a writer whose concern with 'seeing' clearly is one that good writers have dwelt on over the ages.[5] His comment on existentialism to Susana Onega, quoted in the last chapter, bears repeating, for it shows us what he thought about existentialism only a few years after *Daniel Martin* was published. 'I... am [no] longer an existentialist [either] in the social sense, [or] in the cultural sense', he told her. 'I am really much more interested in what fiction is about.'[6] In *Daniel Martin* the question of what fiction is about turns on the problems a writer must face if seeking to use writing as a means of becoming more authentic, more self-aware, and more clear-sighted in the Arnoldian sense of being able to '[see] life steadily and [see] it whole'.

Significantly, the novel's semi-autobiographical main character, Daniel Martin, never dismisses existentialism altogether.[7] His 'to hell with existentialist nausea', a phrase oft quoted by critics, is uttered in a moment of irritation, a moment in which he also dismisses 'cultural fashion' and 'élitist guilt' (432). Elsewhere, he speaks of existentialism as a philosophy to which he was drawn as a student at Oxford, and to one aspect of which he has returned in middle age, when he gives thought to writing a novel in the interests of recovering his lost authenticity. For he recognises that both he and Jane, the woman he eventually marries, have wandered from the straight and narrow, and need, as Fowles has said, to rediscover a sense of their own authenticity, a sense arising from the autobiographical novel Dan spends much of *Daniel Martin* thinking about.[8]

Daniel Martin is an Englishman in his fifties who has spent much of his working life in Los Angeles as a writer of film scripts. Near the start of the novel we learn that he has reached the point in his life where he has come to feel 'sick of screenplays', and wants to write 'the real history of what I am'. His partner, Jenny, a young woman about the same age as his daughter Caroline, proposes that he write a novel, but Dan protests that 'he wouldn't know where to begin' (20). Jokingly, Jenny takes it upon herself to write a novel about Simon Wolfe, a partly fictional character based on Martin. 'S. Wolfe' is, of course, an anagram of Fowles: Wolfe and Martin are both partly autobiographical, partly

fictional versions of Fowles himself, with Fowles emphasising that all
writers of fiction write from their own experience.

What Jenny writes about Simon Wolfe provides us with some important background information about Dan. From her we learn that he is
divorced, that he has lived in America for some years but prefers his
native England, and that he was once a playwright (his plays, she
comments, were 'square' [45]), but has been writing film scripts for
most of his adult life. If asked to define Dan's 'essence', Jenny says that
she would describe him as being 'Something in transit, hardly ever altogether with you... Not just in transit. Self-contained. Very planned and
compact, like his handwriting' (37–8). Less flattering is Martin's view of
himself. He is all too conscious that the film industry 'distorts the vision
of all who work in it' (147), that his own vision has been corrupted by
his work, and that he has somehow lost touch with his 'true nature'
(169). Accordingly, he has come to think of himself 'as if he were... a
fiction, a paper person in someone else's script' (68); in existential
terms, he has become aware of being inauthentic.

As he reflects on how he might write a 'real history of what I am', he
sees that various problems stand in his way. The first problem is that of
subjectivity. In thinking about his past – about the novel he *might* write –
Martin alternates between first- and third-person narration, for he
wants to present as balanced and objective a view of himself as possible.
He also alternates between the present tense and the past, and while it
is difficult always to be certain why he is writing in one tense or the
other, his use of the present to describe scenes from his childhood
reminds us of David's use of the present in *David Copperfield* to emphasise that his childhood is particularly vivid to his mind.[9] Like David,
Dan describes scene after carefully recollected scene from his childhood, largely in the present tense; where he differs from Dickens's
character is in his frequent changes of narrative viewpoint. We can see
the resemblance to, and an interesting difference from, David's writing
in the closing sentences of the novel's first chapter, where the adult
Martin remembers the boy he once was so vividly that:

> I feel in his pocket and bring out a clasp-knife; plunge the blade in
> the red earth to clean it of the filth from the two rabbits he has
> gutted; slit; liver, intestines, stench. He stands and turns and begins
> to carve his initials on the beech-tree. ...
>   Close shot.

D.H.M.
And underneath: *21 Aug 42.*

Here we have not only the vividness and immediacy of the present-tense childhood sections in *David Copperfield*, but a change from first- to third-person viewpoint, and the use of a standard film technique, a close shot, to bring the scene to an end. Dan uses film techniques throughout *Daniel Martin*, but considers film to be a limited medium, one that 'excludes all but now; permits no glances away to past and future' (168).[10] If he is to recover a sense of his own authenticity, Dan believes that he must do so by writing a novel.

But it is not just a matter of employing the right medium. Dan is aware that, as he grew up, he spent much of his time fending off the influences that would otherwise have made him conventional and inauthentic. Although the son of a vicar, he chooses, at seventeen, to become an atheist, and 'to prove I was no tame victim of my background; [I] swore and blasphemed, swopped filth with the best...' (92). What he is describing here is, of course, the rebellion of an immature adolescent; yet it is clear that in rejecting his father's belief in God, Victorian approach to sexuality, and faith in the social hierarchy, Dan is a young existentialist in the making.

As a student at Oxford, he takes an active interest in existentialism, but it is not until his final year that he commits his first truly existential act. Engaged to a fellow student named Nell, he sleeps with her sister Jane, for no better reason than that Jane is attracted to him, and he to her. 'Our surrender to existentialism and each other was', Dan comments, 'fraught with evil. It defiled the printed text of life; broke codes with a vengeance; and it gave Dan a fatal taste for adultery, for seducing, for playing Jane's part that day' (100). Here Dan assumes the voice and point of view of a conventional moralist – the voice of someone very much like his father – in describing this adolescent act of love as 'evil', in claiming that it 'defiled the printed text of life', and that it gave Dan a 'fatal taste for adultery'. If Dan and Jane were *both* existentialists – if both believed the world to be without moral and spiritual guidelines – they would have freely chosen to go to bed together, untroubled by conventional scruples. But Jane has been preparing to become a Catholic, and is soon to be married to Anthony, a Catholic fellow student. Her growing faith strikes Dan as being 'absurd' (117): she is an intelligent woman, and he is at a loss to understand why she has decided to surrender her independence of thought to a highly prescriptive church. In marrying Anthony, despite the fact that she is more attracted to Dan, Jane believes that she is making a noble sacrifice, as is Dan in marrying Nell. '"We'll always be closer in one way to each other than to them", [Dan said]... [Jane] smiled, then spoke more gravely, "In what we gave up for them"' (115).

In saying this, Jane is giving voice to her belief in the virtue of self-sacrifice, familiar to us from the lives of Catholic martyrs. By the time she meets Dan again in middle age, however, she has renounced her Catholic vows, and is, to quote two famous lines from Arnold's 'Stanzas from the Grande Chartreuse', 'Wandering between two worlds, one dead,/ The other powerless to be born'.[11] At this point in the novel, Jane has left the Christian world behind her, but is as yet 'powerless to be born' into the world of the post-Christian twentieth century. Interestingly, the two lines from Arnold are very close to the novel's epigraph, a quotation from Gramsci's *Prison Notebooks*: 'The crisis consists precisely in the fact that the old is dying and the new cannot be born; in this interregnum a great variety of morbid symptoms appears' ([3]). Where Gramsci speaks of an 'interregnum' between one age and the next, *Daniel Martin* is concerned with the death of nineteenth-century England and the dawning of a new age in 1951, the year that the Festival of Britain was celebrated.[12] The new world that in Arnold and Gramsci is yet to come has its counterpart for Fowles in postwar Britain, a world with which he is familiar, and in which he discerns the 'morbid symptoms' of widespread social illness.

While any number of modern social ills are mentioned in *Daniel Martin*, the one that Fowles takes most seriously is the failure of individuals to seek a sense of their own authenticity. On his deathbed, Anthony says that although he is 'still defeated by the conundrum of God', it is clear to him that evil is 'Not seeing whole' (196). Thus, when Jane chooses to surrender herself to Catholicism rather than work out a system of beliefs of her own, she acts inauthentically, failing, in Arnold's phrase, to 'see life steadily and see it whole'. Later she flirts, again inauthentically, with the idea of joining the Communist Party – of embracing a body of political dogma rather than developing her own political beliefs. The terminally ill Anthony sees that he has inflicted an equally serious 'illness' on Jane by insisting that she conform to his Catholic outlook. Shortly before his death, he entreats Dan to 'help disinter the person Jane might have been from beneath the person she now is' (191). Dan is puzzled by the request, but finally agrees to it, not only in the interests of helping Jane, but of bringing to an end the inauthentic life he has been living since his divorce from Nell.

At this point in the novel, Dan takes on the role of 'magus', serving Jane very much as Conchis does Nicholas in Fowles's second published novel. He differs from Conchis, however, in that he has not yet shed his own inauthenticity; he therefore spends as much time guiding *himself* in the direction of greater authenticity as he does Jane. By the end of the novel, Dan sees more clearly than before the extent to which he is a product of his age, nationality and social class, these three being, for both Fowles and his character, important influences on whether or not a given individual manages to attain to authenticity.

Having shown us, early in the novel, how he rebelled against the Victorian religious faith, views on sexuality and the social hierarchy, Dan comments that 'Thorncombe [the rural house he has bought] must be partly a product of my own history and genetic make-up... [and of the fact that] I am English' (80). Throughout the novel, he is concerned both with how his background can be a barrier to achieving authenticity, and yet how, paradoxically, it can also be an important part of what it means to be authentic. Thus, although he has worked in America for many years, and is (as Jenny observes) 'permanently mid-Atlantic' in some ways, he still clings to his 'accent and idiom' (38): being English is an important aspect of who he really is.

'I am', says Dan, reflecting on what is to be middle class, English, and of a particular age and generation, 'trying to exculpate myself, not explain cultures' (80). What he means by this is not clear until later in the novel, when he says that at the end of World War Two, Britain put its age-old (but largely Victorian) notions of duty, national prestige and spurious uniformity behind it, replacing them with a new dedication to self. 'The age', says Dan, commenting on himself in the third person, 'offered him old sins he could convert into supposed new freedoms' (171): his selfish behaviour to Nell and various other women is consistent with the selfishness of the times. His wish to 'exculpate' himself is thus a wish to show that he could not have behaved otherwise; but this, of course, is inconsistent with being authentic, for the authentic individual is one who has discovered his true nature, and has in the process thrown off the shackles of a conventional upbringing, enabling himself to behave with complete freedom of will.

What Dan has to say about the Victorian period and about General Kitchener, the subject of a filmscript he is writing, helps us to see this more clearly. The Victorian period, Dan says, was characterised by 'Britishness', which he takes to be an 'obsession with patriotism, duty, national destiny, the sacrifice of all personal temperament and inclination... to an external system: Empire. Empire was the great disease... and profoundly un-English... The true England was freedom to be self, to stay unattached to anything, except transiently, but the drifting freedom' (450). To be British, Dan implies, is to sacrifice one's identity to the greater good of Empire: it is to be a figure like Kitchener. Caught up in the need to present a conventional front at all times, Kitchener surrendered his authenticity, with the result that 'his inner soul [became] devious, convoluted, far more tyrannized by his own personal myth than the public one he appeared to be building' (451).[13] In other words, Kitchener's conventional 'Britishness' – his devotion to duty and national destiny – stifled his 'Englishness', his freedom to be himself.

Significantly, Dan departs from existential teaching in holding that it is impossible to be completely free. In the course of his life, he has veered, he says, 'between a belief in at least a degree of free will and in a determinism' (169), indicating that the experience of achieving authenticity is not accompanied, for him, by that of attainment to unalloyed freedom.[14] 'The only clear conclusion I have come to', he says, 'is that what have appeared to be my own freely taken decisions provide very little evidence of more wisdom than the blind dictates of destiny' (169). What have appeared to be freely taken decisions may in fact have been determined by forces beyond Dan's control: if it is doubtful that an individual *can* be free, the experience of becoming authentic is not necessarily accompanied by that of accession to unalloyed freedom. The one certain thing, Dan believes, about attaining to authenticity is that one comes to know 'what one's true nature is' (169). And this accounts for his interest in the question of what it is to be English – a question Fowles has said is at the heart of the novel[15] – for knowing what it *means* to be English is an essential step towards achieving self-knowledge.

Dan believes writing to be the key to self-discovery, and fiction to be a better genre than drama for the purpose, because fiction is 'very

English', while 'the theatre (despite Shakespeare) is not' (171). The English, he says, are a private, discreet people, and 'the stage is... nearer an indecent reality than [fiction]. It tells secrets publicly, it gabs to strangers, its lines are spoken not by anonymous print... merely in the single mind, but by men and women in front of an audience' (171). Drama is too public, and film is no better:

> For us English the camera, the public eye, invites performance, lying. We make abundant use of these appearances in our comedy, ...but for our private reality we go elsewhere, and above all, to words. Since we are careful to reveal our true selves only in private, the 'private' form of the read text must suit us better than the publicity of the seen spectacle. ...[Any] true picture of the English must express what the camera cannot capture... (292)

While Dan's plan to write a novel about his innermost experiences is reminiscent of Marcel's at the end of *A la recherche du temps perdu*, he allies himself not with Proust, but with (and this is at first sight a little surprising) the quintessentially English Robin Hood. 'I... sensed a far greater capacity for retreat in fiction. In Robin Hood terms I saw in it a forest, after the thin copse of the filmscript' (294).[16] For Dan, film is too superficial to serve as a means to self-discovery; to achieve worthwhile, in-depth results, it is important to write fiction instead.

Writing fiction in the interests of discovering truths about himself poses certain problems, problems that Dan recognises the need to solve. We have already seen that he is concerned with the problem of objectivity, and seeks to solve it partly by alternating between first-person and third-person points of view. Another solution is to delegate part of the writing to Jenny, his much younger girl friend. In the chapter entitled 'An Unbiased View', Jenny describes Simon Wolfe – her fictionalised version of Dan – as a man who is inclined to play roles: that of 'a character out of Hemingway', for example, or 'the man in *Under the Volcano*' (36). But if Dan plays roles, he is unaware of it: throughout the novel, he makes every effort to avoid being inauthentic. Jenny thinks of him as a Mr Knightley figure, and of herself as a kind of Emma, but this turns out to be a fantasy that Dan has not shared. When he reveals that he has decided to leave her for Jane, Jenny says bitterly,

'I don't think you're my Mr Knightley at all.'
'Never one of my ambitions.'
'You're not even trying.'
'Because you aren't an Emma.' (454)

In assuming the role of Jane Austen's Emma, Jenny, like Miranda in *The Collector* before her, clearly indicates that she is inauthentic – that she is given to playing roles rather than devoted to seeking her true self. Miranda assigns G.P. the part of Mr Knightley, and Clegg that of Mr Elton. '[I'll] be like Emma', she fantasises, 'and arrange a marriage for him, and with happier results. Some little Harriet Smith, with whom he could be mousy and sane and happy' (*The Collector*, 224). Jenny would similarly like to arrange a marriage for herself with Dan, but it is clear that it would not be a marriage of equals.

At the time of Anthony's death, Dan prefers Jenny's company to Jane's, partly for the obvious reason that he has long been out of touch, and partly because the younger Jenny is superficially more attractive. But as he reacquaints himself with Jane, it becomes clear to him that she stands a far better chance of becoming authentic than Jenny does. When he takes Jenny to visit the ancient Indian settlement at Tsankawi, in New Mexico, he is dismayed at her philistine attitude to the artefacts they find there: the shards that, in his view, bear testimony to Tsankawi's ability to defeat time and death, are for her no more than pretty objects to be strung on silver wire and given to friends as necklaces. With varicose veins and other signs of middle age, Jane is less obviously attractive than Jenny; yet Dan finds her more interesting, because she is someone who has for years been in the habit of 'search[ing] for the reality behind the tailor's dummy' (361). She is someone who wants to go beyond appearances, beyond the inauthentic, in search of the authenticity that comes only to the intelligent Few.

Jane's marriage to Anthony has, however, been less than satisfactory, for it has influenced her to make some inauthentic decisions. In retrospect, Jane recognises that she converted to Catholicism after marrying Anthony because the Catholic church offered the means, it seemed, of solving all her problems. Yet, although conscious of having wakened up 'twenty-five years too late to what [she is]' (413) – in existential terms, inauthentic – she still flirts with the idea of joining the Communist Party, and having all her problems solved for her there, too, rather than seek her own solutions. Her tendency to find love and acceptance in groups of people – groups like the Catholic Church and the Communist Party – and to be shy of expressing her love for an individual man, derives, as she tells Dan, from the fact that she was denied love as a child. What Dan must do is wean her away from her reliance on groups, and help her both to know and love herself as a prerequisite to loving him.

He is, however, at a disadvantage – that of being only a little further down the road towards authenticity than she is – which means that he is less than an expert on what needs to be done to help Jane become authentic. And oddly enough, by lending him a book of essays by Georg Lukács, the Marxist literary critic, Jane helps him to move closer to becoming authentic. As they have sailed down the Nile, Dan has returned to thinking about the novel he has been planning to write, and finds that he now wants to present himself in the 'passive third person', as 'one' (548). He is, of course, trying to be objective about himself, as earlier in the novel; but for the first time he is also attempting to come to terms with a comment in one of Lukács's essays. In a passage that Dan finds particularly impressive, Lukács asks, 'is man the helpless victim of transcendental and inexplicable forces, or is he a member of a human community in which he can play a part, however small, towards its modification and reform?' (532). On reading this, Dan feels convinced that he and Jane have been behaving 'like someone else's – or something else's – creatures... Not saying what we really think. Not really judging for our true selves' (603). It is not, Dan reflects, just he and Jane, but their whole 'generation, age, [and] century' that have 'gone wrong' (610), so that instead of being Lukácsian members of 'a human community in which they can play a part', the unreflective members of that generation are condemned to 'the tedium of the treadmill, the horror of existence passed so, like caged animals' (611).

Dan would like to think of himself as being a member, not of the unreflective Many, but of the intelligent, independent-minded Few. What prevents him from being free is the attitude he shares with the rest of his generation, which for him is summed up by

> the [large number of] mirrors in his student room; the overweening narcissism of all their generation... all the liberal scruples, the oncern with living right and doing right, were not based on external principles, but self-obsession (630).

It is only by becoming aware of this narcissistic self-obsession in his generation, but more importantly, in himself, that Dan is able to act with some measure of freedom. Returning to existentialist teaching, he decides that 'right feeling' (646), or 'instinct' (647), terms that appear to be synonymous with 'authenticity', are all-important. It is only when we learn to cast off conventional ideas and opinions, and be guided by instinct, that we will begin, Dan says, to act freely.

Fowles never allows us to enter Jane's mind: we become privy to some of her private thoughts in her conversations with Dan, but are not allowed to witness the working of her mind at first hand. As Dan spends more and more time with her, however, he sees that beneath 'all her faults, her wrong dogmas, ...there lay, as there had always lain... that mysterious sense he had always thought of as right feeling' (646). Jane has the capacity for 'right feeling', or 'instinct', but even at a fairly late point in the novel, has been unable to act on it as fully as she might. What changes things for her is an incident in Palmyra, Lebanon, where she watches a scrawny desert bitch try to lure Dan and herself away from a litter of pups. While she is watching the bitch, Dan stands behind, at some distance, watching Jane, who, except for the fact that she is seated, is to all appearances the woman who prompted Fowles to write *Daniel Martin*. Watching Jane, Dan is unable to tell what she is thinking. As we later discover, however, Jane has been reflecting on the need to respond more to her instincts, and less to attitudes learned from her dalliance with Catholicism, which (in her view) provides support for people who fear love; and with Communism, whose generalised love for fellow man she has used as a substitute for love of any individual man.[17] Jane's transformation in this scene brings her closer, at long last to Dan.

In the final pages of the novel, Dan, having returned to England, explains to Jenny his decision to drop her in favour of Jane, who has accepted his proposal of marriage. Jenny is understandably upset, and accuses him of being 'a devious, lying bastard' (655); Dan is convinced, nevertheless, that he has made the right choice in Jane, and as we leave the novel, we are secure in the knowledge that he will marry her. Many readers of *Daniel Martin* feel a pang of regret that Dan chooses to reject Jenny: the problem, of course, is that Jenny has revealed herself much more fully to us than Jane, by writing episodes in the Simon Wolfe novel, and is therefore a more sympathetic character. Here she comes across as intelligent, attractive and kindly – though elsewhere she strikes us as being rather philistine in her attitude to the Tsankawi shards, and as a choice Dan has made not out of 'right feeling' but largely out of lust. In the novel's closing pages, he tells Jenny that he will continue to write the Simon Wolfe novel, and it comes as a surprise to us that he tells Jane, on the last page, that

he had found a last sentence for the novel he was never going to write. She laughed at such flagrant Irishry; which is perhaps why, in the end, and in the knowledge that Dan's novel can never be read, lies eternally in the future, his ill-concealed ghost has made that impossible last his own impossible first. (668)

Just as, earlier in the novel, Fowles has reminded us that Dan and Jane are 'someone else's… creatures' (603) – namely his own – so he emphasises here that Dan is no more than a fictional creation, and will never complete the novel that he has begun. The 'ill-concealed ghost' behind his writing is, of course, Fowles himself, whose ghostly non-appearance in *Daniel Martin* contrasts with his two major entries into *The French Lieutenant's Woman* as a fictional character. The first sentence of *Daniel Martin* reads 'Whole sight; or all the rest is desolation' (7). What Fowles wants us to understand is that it is important not just for Dan and Jane to strive for 'whole sight', for what might be otherwise termed 'right feeling': it is also important for all the intelligent members of Dan's generation, and indeed for every member of the Few at all times in history. For it is only as we begin to achieve 'whole sight', 'right feeling' or existential authenticity, that it is possible for us to realise our human potential.

7

A Maggot

Fowles's most recent novel, *A Maggot*, is set in 1736, a year, as he says in the preface,

> very nearly equidistant from 1689, the culmination of the English Revolution, and 1789, the start of the French; in a sort of dozing solstitial standstill, a stasis of the kind predicted by those today who see all evolution as a punctuated equilibrium, between those two zenith dates and all they stand for; ...at a time of reaction from the intemperate extremisms of the previous century, yet already hatching the seeds of the world-changing upheaval to come. (16)

Poised between two revolutions, 1736 is a year in which were 'already hatching the seeds' of not only the French Revolution but (as Fowles has said elsewhere) of the Romantic Movement, the two being for him part of 'the same phenomenon'.[1] Moreover, during the 'dozing solstitial standstill' of which 1736 is a part, various religious groups claiming the authority of divine revelation were formed, one of the best known being the Shakers. But the Shakers and the Romantic Movement are not Fowles's only interests, for the question of how *A Maggot* departs from the conventions of historical fiction also looms large – the question of how and why Fowles's most recent work is 'a maggot' rather than a conventional historical novel.

'A maggot is the larval stage of a winged creature', says the author in the first sentence of the preface, but 'an older though now obsolete sense of the word is that of whim or quirk'(5).[2] *A Maggot* is whimsical in that it arose from an image that came unexpectedly to Fowles's mind, of a small group of riders making their way over a deserted landscape. At first the travellers were faceless; in time, however, one of them began to take on the features of a nameless young woman in a portrait Fowles had acquired, dated 16 July 1683. 'This precise dating', he says, 'pleased me at first as much as the drawing itself, which is not of any distinction; yet something in the long dead girl's face, in her eyes, an inexplicable presentness, a refusal to die, came slowly to haunt me'(5).

A Maggot is a quirk in that it very largely abandons conventional narration in favour of a question-and-answer format. The questions issue from Henry Ayscough, a solicitor intent on solving the mystery of a young aristocrat's disappearance; the answers are given by some of the last people to see the young man alive.

'Before I wrote *A Maggot*', Fowles told James Baker in 1986,

> I tried to work out why I particularly liked old murder and treason trials, whatever they might be, ...and decided it was because they left out one important branch of novel writing, which is describing how people look and what they do: you know, 'He opened the window, lit a cigarette, had another whiskey', or whatever it is. ...So that was the main reason for that choice; trying to prove I can do with one arm, what, in the past, I've done with both.[3]

For Fowles it was a challenge to write a novel in which we *hear* the characters rather than see them, and in which we learn from their answers to questions only what we might expect to learn from witnesses under oath. Thus we are made privy to *events*, for the most part, rather than intimate feelings, and at times are denied answers when Ayscough's questions are too personal. Fowles's overall purpose is to impress on us the difficulties involved in being certain about something that happened even a short time ago. Larval when he first conceived it, *A Maggot* takes flight in the reader's imagination as it becomes more and more apparent that the disappearance is impossible to explain in wholly rational terms.[4]

As a background to writing the novel, Fowles read a variety of seventeenth- and eighteenth-century texts, including John Aubrey's *Monumenta Britannica*, which contains information about how the eighteenth century viewed Stonehenge, and Pastor Moritz's *Travels in England in 1782*, from which derive both the town of C– and the cavern in which Rebecca experiences 'June Eternal'.[5] He also reproduced passages from *The Gentleman's Magazine* of 1736 in *A Maggot*, in the interests of fostering a sense of what life was like in the early eighteenth century. Finally, he worked through all of Fielding's plays and read a late seventeenth-century comedy by Sir Thomas Otway entitled *The Soldier's Fortune*.[6] This last work was of particular interest because, Fowles has said, it uses 'all the slang of the prostitutes and libertines and gentlemen of London in its period. Otway's dialogue is so vivid that it gives you an extraordinary insight into important aspects of [late] seventeenth century life...'[7]

Yet, despite his efforts to create as vivid a sense of the times as possible, Fowles emphasises that he would prefer *A Maggot* not to be seen 'as a historical novel'(6). 'I don't like [historical] novels', he told James Baker, 'where you feel that you are being lectured to by a history professor who is accurately reflecting some kind of general view, speaking for all reasonable mankind.'[8] To Robert Foulke, he spoke of being drawn to

> the rather old-fashioned narrative historians of the past, with all their prejudices and idiosyncrasies, [rather than] to the highly scientific historiographical studies that proliferate in the modern academy. I'm not saying that sort of thing doesn't ever produce useful results, but I don't get much pleasure or serious edification from a long list of graphs or statistics. For me, history is a form of literature, or should be, and good historians are in many ways closer to the novelist than other kinds of writers.[9]

History is a form of literature partly in the sense that historians 'like to claim that they always work from the facts, ...[when] there's so much in history we don't really know.'[10] In the absence of facts, the would-be historian has no choice but to become a judicious writer of fiction. 'I've just done a little booklet... on medieval life', Fowles told Foulke, 'and realised early on it would have to be done as fiction, more or less, because we have really very few facts that we can rely upon.'[11]

Fiction is not only a necessary part of recorded history, but also an analogue to it. Like the historian, who, after surveying what is known about a sequence of events, works out a summary and interpretation of them, so the conventional novelist creates the illusion that he or she is surveying and interpreting the activities of some real people who actually behaved in the ways the novel describes. Often the novelist pretends to know everything there is to know about these 'people', but authorial omniscience is, Fowles says, no more than 'a pretence, ...a common trick writers use, to suggest that they know everything... [when] it seems to me much more honest to say, "This is my personal opinion".'[12]

With this last statement, Fowles takes us back to his comments on authorial omniscience in *The French Lieutenant's Woman*. Conventional omniscient narration is unacceptable in the twentieth century, he argues there, because it is inappropriate for a contemporary novelist to pretend that he is an analogue to God in a century characterised by scepticism and doubt. The pretence that an author knows everything about the characters he creates must be exposed for what it is, since in real life, no one knows everything there is to know about other individuals, no matter how close they are to them. An author may create the *illusion* that he or she is capable of commenting omnisciently on the events in a given fiction, but it is (and can be) no more than that – an illusion.

Fowles's dissatisfaction with conventional omniscient narration is most evident in the introductory section of *A Maggot*, which focuses on a night spent by five travellers in the West Country town of C–. Throughout, he uses the present tense rather than the past, as if to suggest that his characters' future is something that he has not yet witnessed and is therefore unable to reveal to us. In addition, he makes it clear that he knows no more about the novel's characters than anyone else who might have met them on the road for the first time.[13] Whether Bartholomew and Lacy are truly nephew and uncle, whether Dick and Rebecca are (as they first appear to be), 'journeyman and wife chance-met' (8), whether Lacy is truly an 'actor' (25), and whether the story he and the other characters tell the innkeeper about why they are travelling westwards is correct, are some of the many questions that are left unanswered until much later in the novel.

It is consistent with his denial of conventional omniscience that Fowles refuses to reveal his characters' thoughts in the novel's opening section. He says, for example, of Dick, that he has

a strangely inscrutable face, which does not reveal whether its expressionlessness is that of an illiterate stupidity, an ignorant acceptance of destiny, ...or whether it hides something deeper, some resentment of grace, some twisted sectarian suspicion of personable young women who waste time picking flowers... [His] eyes add greatly to the impression of inscrutability, ...for they betray no sign of emotion, seem always to stare, to suggest that their owner is somewhere else. So might twin camera lenses see, not normal human eyes. (11)

A conventionally omniscient narrator might have told us what Dick's inscrutable expression hides, why his eyes betray no sign of emotion, whether he is truly a resentful, twisted member of a sect, and what conclusions we should draw from the mention of camera lenses in a novel set in the early eighteenth century. By contrast, Fowles plays the role of a less-than-omniscient, twentieth-century observer of life in the year 1736 – just as in *The French Lieutenant's Woman*, he acts as a less-than-omniscient observer of life in 1867. In each case, he presents us not with a historical novel but a 'maggot' – a subjective, idiosyncratic, fictionalised view of the past.

What this means in more detail becomes clear from a careful examination of two of the novel's most important anomalies. The first is the birth date of the real Ann Lee, which comes some two months *before* Rebecca Lee and Dick Thurlow, whom Fowles would have us believe are her mother and father, had ever met. 'Readers who know something of what that Manchester baby was to become in the real world', comments Fowles in the epilogue, 'will not need telling how little this is a historical novel. ...I know nothing in reality of her mother, and next to nothing of various other characters, such as Lacy and Wardley, who also come from real history.' What we may have accepted as historical portraiture, then, turns out to be 'almost all invention' (455).

The second anomaly concerns the last place that the travellers stop for the night. Although it is easy to follow their route on a map from London to Devon, the last place they stop, C–, is, as Pierre Monnin has observed, 'impossible to locate on any map (no matter how detailed), or to identify in any guidebook for the district'.[14] Here what seems to be a real town, C–, a town real enough for the Bristol lawyer, Richard Pygge, to visit, and to ride to the cavern nearby, does not exist. It is a fiction based on Castleton, in Derbyshire, a town visited by Pastor Moritz, many miles away.[15] We must not accept too readily that everything that appears to be objective fact is necessarily that, for far from being a straightforward historical novel, *A Maggot* is 'not an attempt, either in fact or in language, to reproduce known history' (455); instead, it is a novel characterised by vagueness, uncertainty and mystery.

As we saw in Chapter 5, Fowles once remarked to an interviewer that 'Mystery... lies in things and in gaps in the story. ...I regard all that in books as symbolic of the general mystery in cosmic... terms.'[16] An element of that 'general mystery' is to be found in *The Gentleman's Magazine* excerpts, where we may imagine that we are being presented with objective truth about the early eighteenth century when, often, nothing could be less certain. There is no reason to doubt the statement in the April number, for example, that William Bithell and William Morgan were hanged at Worcester 'for cutting down *Ledbury* Turnpikes' (59), or that the other men mentioned in other numbers were hanged for crimes our own century would consider trivial. But what are we to make of some of the magazine's truly bizarre stories – for example the one in the October number, about a peculiar fish thrown ashore in Devon? It is '4 Foot long', *The Gentleman's Magazine* tells us, 'has a Head like a Toad, 2 feet like a Goose and the Mouth opens 12 Inches wide' (409). Did this freak of nature really exist? Are we truly to believe that 'One of this Kind was dissected at the College of Physicians in the presence of K. *Charles* II'? (409). Or is this just a rather juicy story some journalist made up in order to sell magazines?

The only way we could be certain whether this story is true would be to compare it with whatever first-hand accounts of the fish have survived. If there are no first-hand accounts extant, or if the surviving accounts (whether first- or second-hand) are unreliable, we would be obliged to accept that this story is a minor mystery which, together with a host of other mysteries, both major and minor, contributes to the enormous 'general mystery' posed by the world at large. It is important to bear this in mind, for the unanswered (and ultimately unanswerable) question of his Lordship's disappearance, together with the many other mysteries in the fictional parts of *A Maggot*, are, as Fowles has said, 'symbolic of the general mystery in cosmic... terms'.

Significantly, in seeking to solve the mystery surrounding the young aristocrat, Ayscough, solicitor to the young man's father, uses much the same approach as an academic historian would. Typically, a historian interested in answering questions about a given event in the past would begin by examining the written testimony of people who had lived during that time. Aware that this testimony might be subjective or distorted, the historian would glean from it whatever facts – dates, names, places – are common to all or most of them, and would use these facts as the basis on which to write a history of what happened. In like kind, Ayscough seeks testimony concerning his Lordship's disappearance from witnesses who were with him, and is clearly aware of the importance of distinguishing between subjective testimony and objective fact. 'There are two truths', says his clerk at one point, clearly echoing Ayscough himself. 'One that a person believes is truth; and one that is truth incontestible' (348). Ayscough seeks the latter truth about the missing young man, but in spite of his efforts, 'truth incontestible' eludes him, just as, more generally, incontestible knowledge of the world and its mysteries will always elude human inquiry.

As we read *A Maggot*, we sympathise with the lawyer, for we share his desire to discover what happened to the young man who has disappeared, and see that he has good reasons for keeping his witnesses firmly under his thumb. Unsurprisingly, Ayscough is at his most effective early in the novel, when dealing with the likes of Puddicombe, Jones and Lacy, for these are the kinds of men he would be used to questioning as witnesses in court. Thus, he rightly reminds Puddicombe that all his testimony must be based on what he knows of his 'own eyes and ears' (66), and not what he has heard from other people, for hearsay evidence has no validity in a court of law. His abruptness to Jones might seem ill-mannered, but it can be justified on the grounds that Jones is a petty rogue and liar, and needs to be chivvied into telling the truth. Much of what the Welshman has to say is of little value, however, for although it has to do with the all-important question of what happened to Rebecca, Dick and his Lordship in the cavern, his testimony is based on information obtained from Rebecca, who later confesses frankly that she 'lied' (329) to Jones.

Of the three men, Lacy is by far the best witness, for as Katherine Tarbox has observed, 'he is honest, forthright, and his memory is preternaturally sharp – a result of his actor's training'.[17] Moreover, Lacy is the one member of the group to whom his Lordship confides his theories about mathematics, Stonehenge, and the importance of searching for one's 'life's meridian'. The young man, says Lacy, believes that there is a

divine cipher that all living things must copy, for that the ratio between its successive numbers was that also of a secret of the Greeks, who did discover a perfect proportion, I believe he said it to be of one to one and six tenths. He pointed to all that chanced about us, and said, that these numbers might be read therein; and cited other examples, …[which] accorded with the order of petals and leaves in trees and herbs, I know not what. (146)

While this idea is partly a variation on Pythagorean theory, it also suggests that his Lordship is a Romantic before his time, for the idea that God is immanent in nature is central to Wordsworth, one of the major poets of the Romantic Movement.[18] The young aristocrat knows nothing, of course, of a movement that is to begin some sixty years in the future. What intrigues him is the thought that the ancient Druids, credited by the eighteenth century with the construction of Stonehenge, were aware of the divine cipher 'before Rome, before Christ himself' (149).[19] 'These ancients', he tells Lacy, 'knew a secret I should give all I possess to secure. They knew their life's meridian, and I still search mine. In all else they lived in darkness, …yet this great light they had; while I live in light, and stumble after phantoms' (148–9).

What his Lordship means by 'their life's meridian' is not clear; when Lacy is asked what he took it to mean, he replies, 'Why, sir, no more than is conveyed by any such obscure and fanciful metaphor. It may be, some certainty of belief or faith. I fear he found little consolation in religion as we see it practised in this land' (169). Adding to this statement the fact that 'meridian' can mean either 'the period of greatest vigour [or] splendour', or 'the point at which a sun or star attains its highest altitude', we can gain some idea, at least, of what is intended.[20] In *The Enigma of Stonehenge* Fowles points out that the stones there are an elaborate measuring device to determine 'the two pairs of solstitial and equinoctial dates, climaxes of the four seasons'.[21] What his Lordship appears to be searching for is the moment at which his life will be at its highest splendour – the moment corresponding (metaphorically) to the summer solstice, when the sun in the northern hemisphere is at its highest point in the sky. Unfortunately, Lacy is unable to relate his Lordship's theories to what happens to the young man later in the cavern, for he leaves the group at C–. From Rebecca's testimony, however, it would seem that his Lordship enters the cavern in the hope that the people (or beings) he is to meet there will help him achieve some sort of transcendental religious experience.

In his dealings with the witnesses who precede Rebecca, Ayscough has played the part of a petty tyrant, threatening Jones, for example, with a flogging and Lacy with the gallows: from these two, as from the others he has questioned, the lawyer has commanded the respect that comes of fear. Unlike the earlier witnesses, however, Rebecca refuses to be intimidated. She is unafraid to protest that some of his questions touch on areas that are none of his business (in which case she refuses to answer them), and she tells him frankly that the language, or 'alphabet' (317) he uses, prevents him from accepting a truth that transcends 'truth incontestible': the truth of religious revelation.

A rational, sceptical man, Ayscough bases his distinction between objective fact and subjective distortion on common-sense grounds. Indeed, his many common-sensical objections to the extravagant testimony of some witnesses – Jones in particular – earn him the special sympathy of the reader anxious to solve the mystery of his Lordship's disappearance, for it seems that the lawyer's down-to-earth approach will ultimately reveal all. But what is common sense to one age – in this case, the Age of Reason – is not always so to another. Ayscough is very much a man of his time, and although his rational, sceptical manner has considerable appeal when he questions the characters who profess the conventional beliefs of the established church, his conservatism and fear of unbridled religious emotion make him more sceptical of Rebecca's experience of Stonehenge, and later of June Eternal, than a sophisticated twentieth-century reader might be.

As she begins to tell of her experience at Stonehenge, of seeing a young man and an old man standing together, bathed in a bright light emanating from above, Ayscough accuses her of lying, and listens sceptically when she insists she is telling the truth. The two men 'lived', she protests. 'They were no dream nor vision' (326). When the lawyer expresses further scepticism, and asks her pointedly what his Lordship's purpose in all this could have been, Rebecca replies that 'His Lordship had more than one purpose, and one a far greater' (336). It was one of his aims, she thinks, to persuade her to abandon her life as a prostitute. 'You are she I have sought' (328), he says at Stonehenge, and here it seems apparent to the reader (though not immediately to Rebecca) that she has been the goal of a mission undertaken by his Lordship, a mission whose purpose is to enable a reformed sinner and a man of kind heart but limited abilities to serve as father and mother to Ann Lee, one of the founding members of the Shakers.[22]

Rebecca's account of what happened in the cavern places a great strain on Ayscough's credulity, for she tells first of a woman whose clothes are quite unlike those worn in the eighteenth century, then of 'a great swollen maggot, white as snow upon the air' (359). It is not until she reveals that the latter 'was no true maggot nor living creature, but something of artifice, a machine or engine' (364), and that it was 'not of flesh, as it were wood-japanned, or fresh-tinned metal, large as three coaches end to end' (359), that the lawyer can begin to take her seriously. Even so, he feels obliged to ask whether 'this was some engine... that might mount into the heavens, as a bird?' (363). To the twentieth-century reader it is clear that the maggot may be a spaceship, and the strangely-dressed people (or beings) either aliens from some other planet, or time-travellers returned from the future to observe history in the making. But to Ayscough, who knows nothing of either spaceships or time travel, the maggot seems to resemble a chariot of the Lord – though Rebecca emphasises that it bore 'no alphabet letters, nor numbers, [nor] emblem of Christianity' (361), and that it has 'no wheels, nor wings, nor horses' (363).

She also says that as she watched the maggot, she was aware that there was a special smell in the air, a smell she identifies as that of 'life eternal' (362). Characteristically, Ayscough demands to know more precisely what she means, and is only satisfied when she says it is like the smell of a virgin rose, 'which a bride must carry in her posy, if she is wed within its season' (362). Here Rebecca is hinting that in the cavern she became in some sense wedded to Christ, just as elsewhere she intimates that she shares in some way in Christ's divinity. 'Thee knows't not who thee mocks' (365), she tells Ayscough, echoing Christ's 'Father, forgive them; for they know not what they do'.[23] In addition, when she tells the lawyer that there will be a Second Coming of Christ, and that the Son of God will return in the form of a baby girl, she hints that she may be the mother of the girl in question. 'She I carry, yea, she shall be more than I, I am but brought to bring her'. Yet she adds that she is neither 'worthy' nor 'vain' (421) enough to be certain that the child she bears will be the agent of the Second Coming. In the remainder of the novel, Fowles toys with the reader's expectations of what is to come: it is only in the epilogue that he reveals that Ann Lee's date of birth was too early for her mother and father to have been Rebecca Lee and Dick Thurlow, his two fictional characters. This is our last reminder that his novel is a 'maggot', rather than a work of fiction that adheres faithfully to established historical fact.

While still in the cavern, Rebecca experiences June Eternal as a place
to which she walks 'out of this cruel world and all its evil, out of my own
most miserable sins and vanity' (378). Ayscough believes that the juice
she, Dick and his Lordship have been given to drink by the people in
the cavern is a potion that has caused her to hallucinate. That may of
course be true, though for the twentieth-century reader, it is also
possible that Rebecca's experience of June Eternal is that of watching a
film or videotape. The important thing, in any case, is that June Eternal
is depicted as an ideal society – one in which people of all races live
together in peace, in which 'spiritual cleanliness' (372) is valued, in
which there are 'no poor, no beggars, no cripples, no sick, not one who
starved... [and] no sign of war, nor destruction, nor cruelty, nor envy
neither; but life eternal' (375). When Rebecca says that 'this land...
worship[s] cleanliness of spirit' (372), that it harbours 'no married
couples, no lovers' (374), and that it features a Holy Trinity not in the
form of Father, Son and Holy Spirit, but of Father, Son and 'Holy
Mother Wisdom' (379), we see that June Eternal closely conforms to
Shaker belief; Fowles has said, in fact, that June Eternal is meant to
portray what the Shaker communities in America would be like.[24]

Having witnessed the possibility of an ideal Christian community,
Rebecca then sees humanity at its worst, in its practice of 'torture, of
murther and treachery, of the slaughter of innocents... and the cruelty
of man more savage than the wildest beasts' (381). As she watches with
horror this spectacle of human suffering (and in particular, the unre-
lieved suffering of 'a girl-child of fourteen' [381]), Rebecca undergoes a
mystical transformation. This involves shedding the harlot/self she once
was and preparing to assume a fresh identity in the light of what she
has experienced in the cavern. When she is returned to the everyday
world, it is in a state of both physical and spiritual nakedness,
suggesting that the old identity has been stripped away, but that the
new one is not yet ready to be donned. She recalls that, at one moment,
Holy Mother Wisdom was at her side, but that at the next, 'she was
departed and I most sore bereft, of worse than my clothes, my soul cast
naked back in this present world' (384).

Interestingly, this statement echoes a passage in Book IV of
Wordsworth's *The Prelude*:

>   . . . Gently did my soul
> Put off her veil, and, self-transmuted, stood

Naked as in the presence of her God.
As on I walked, a comfort seemed to touch
A heart that had not been disconsolate:
Strength came where weakness was not known to be,
At least not felt; and restoration came
Like an intruder knocking at the door
Of unacknowledged weariness.[25]

It is clear that Fowles uses this passage less as a source than as a point of departure for his description of Rebecca's experience, for although her soul puts off its veil and stands 'Naked as in the presence of her God', she has had neither 'A heart that had not been disconsolate', nor a weakness that 'was not known to be', nor an 'unacknowledged weariness', as in the above passage. On the contrary, she has long been aware of the sinfulness of her work as a prostitute. 'I knew I was on the path to hell', she tells Ayscough, speaking of her time at Claiborne's, 'and with no excuse save my own obstinacy in sin...' (309). It is when she starts reading the Bible that she sees that 'what I did was great sin... Still could I not bring myself to do what... I came to see I must. I stayed too fond of worldly things' (310).

Her visionary experience at Stonehenge, however, forces her to confront the wickedness of her life, and fills her with a resolve that she 'should never more be whore...' (324). It is his Lordship who has provided the means by which she reaches this conclusion, a fact that recalls to mind her comment that at Claiborne's she began to look to the young man to provide the 'key' (309) that would release her from the prison of prostitution. What form she expected this 'key' to take is never specified; if she entertained the hope that the young man might marry her, or at the very least, make her his mistress, she does not say as much to Ayscough. In any case, it is her second visionary experience – her experience in the cavern, also made possible by his Lordship, though even more extraordinary than the one at Stonehenge – that radically changes her life. Here, when her vision of June Eternal comes to an end, and she is returned to the everyday world both physically and spiritually naked, it is in the awareness that 'I was vain still, still the harlot, I thought only of myself, one scorned and rejected, that had failed a great test upon me. Poor fool, I knelt there on the stone and prayed I might be taken back...' (384). To strip the harlot/self completely away, she must learn to think less about herself and more about others; significantly, her conviction that there must be 'more love' and 'more light' (419) in the world anticipates an important element of Shaker teaching.

Ayscough finds Rebecca's testimony of little help in his efforts to establish what became of his Lordship. Earlier in the novel, the solic- . itor has boasted of his thoroughness: 'I shall find the bottom to [the mystery of his Lordship's disappearance]', he tells Beckford. 'I work slow but I sift small. ...I'll not rest until all's laid bare' (103). But by the time he has heard the testimony of his last witness, Rebecca, Ayscough knows little more than at the outset of his inquiry. In a last-ditch effort to discover the truth, he invites Rebecca to revise her testimony without penalty, but this the former prostitute refuses to do. 'I have told truth in all' (412), she says. When Ayscough persists, her reply is an emphatic 'I will not change' (415); she has told the truth – the truth of God's revelation – and will not go back on it now, no matter what the inducement.

Ayscough, of course, feels frustrated, for his only witness to what happened to his Lordship in the cavern says that the young man exchanged life on earth for life everlasting, and that his servant Dick died to facilitate his master's union with Christ. 'And now do I see,' says Rebecca,

> they were as one in truth, Dick of the carnal and imperfect body, his Lordship of the spirit; such twin natures as we all must hold, in them made outward and a seeming two. And as Jesus Christ's body must die upon the Cross, so must this latterday earthly self, poor unregenerate Dick, die so the other half be saved. I tell thee now again I believe that other self shall be seen no more upon this earth, no not ever as he has been; yet he is not dead, but lives in June Eternal, and is one with Jesus Christ, as I saw. (421)

A practical, rational man, Ayscough persists in trying to extract from Rebecca a more down-to-earth account of his Lordship's disappearance. All his efforts are in vain, however, for what his witness describes is the experience of holy revelation, rather than that of ordinary visual perception. 'What I see with my eyes is of the body carnal, not certain truth', says Rebecca. 'I see no less true or false than thee in carnal seeing, or any other man and woman' (414). The problem, of course, is that it is not her carnal eyes that have witnessed his Lordship's disappearance but the eyes of her spirit, which have been opened by mystical experience.[26] Though Rebecca believes that the visions she has had at Stonehenge and in the cavern are 'certain truth', Ayscough finally sees that such truth is certain only to those to whom it is revealed. What he wants to arrive at is 'truth incontestible' – the kind of truth on which all witnesses would agree – but with Rebecca his sole witness to what happened in the cavern, visionary truth is the only kind he can expect.

Ayscough has his limitations, but he is too fair a man to dismiss her testimony out of hand. In a letter to his Lordship's father, he emphasises that Rebecca told what she thought was the truth, but that it was of little help to the inquiry. Left with no alternative but to speculate, the lawyer suggests that Dick witnessed his master commit suicide in the cavern, ran outside in horror at what had happened, then returned to hide his Lordship's body after Jones and Rebecca had gone. Once he had done that, says Ayscough, the servant hanged himself in despair: 'like the dog in human form that he was, he knew his beloved master dead and wished to live no more' (444).

There are, however, a number of other possible explanations. It may be, for example, that Dick, who is observed to be resentful of his Lordship, betrayed his master to the beings inside the cave, then fled to hang himself as Judas did after betraying Christ. The fact that the servant seems familiar with the country in the immediate vicinity of the cavern, while his Lordship is not, suggests that Dick brought his master to a pre-arranged meeting, then left him to be murdered. In any case, it would appear that his Lordship was drawn to the cavern by the prospect of some sort of gain in knowledge, though whether it is knowledge about his 'life's meridian', June Eternal or, as Ayscough suggests, 'some dark secret of existence' (445) is not clear.

Nor is it clear why Dick, having hanged himself or been hanged, is found with a clump of violets in his mouth. Did he place them in his mouth as a sign that he died of unrequited love for Rebecca, who often held a nosegay of violets as she rode with the servant? Or were they placed in his mouth by the beings in the cavern, who hanged him after disposing of his Lordship? In that case, were the violets meant to be a symbol of the young aristocrat's attainment of life everlasting? Or are all these possibilities too literal? Can it be that the novel's characters are meant to be Jungian constituents of mind, as Carol Barnum and Susana Onega have suggested?[27]

These questions remain unanswered and unanswerable at the end of
the novel, for as we have seen, Fowles's purpose is to represent 'in gaps
in the story something of the general mystery in cosmic... terms.' But
this mystery is in some ways less important than Fowles's observation of
a change in the way human beings view themselves – a change he sees
starting to take place in the 1730s, but only fully materialising at the
end of the century, with the start of the Romantic Movement. In the
novel's introductory section, he says of Rebecca that her 'time has little
power of seeing people other than they are in outward' (55), for she
lives during the Age of Reason, when the individual's feelings and free
will are of less importance than his or her social class and function in
society. 'To us,' comments Fowles,

> such a world would seem abominably prescribed, with personal
> destiny fixed to an intolerable degree, totalitarian in its essence;
> while to its chained humans our present lives would seem incredibly
> fluid, mobile, rich in free will... and above all anarchically, if not
> insanely, driven by self-esteem and self-interest. (55)

Ayscough's failure to accept Rebecca's story about what happened in
the cavern is, then, partly a failure of imagination arising from some of
the prejudices he harbours against members of the lower orders.
Because he fears that the social classes below his own may rebel and
overthrow the established order, he treats their members with a trucu-
lent suspicion. The threats of flogging and hanging that he makes to
Jones and Lacy, respectively, are in the interests of bringing the two
men to heel; his manner towards Mr Beckford, the parson, and to his
employer, the Duke, is very different. To both he is deferential, while to
the Duke he is openly obsequious.

Ayscough is willing to listen to Rebecca, and to accept that she
genuinely believes that her account of what happened in the cavern is
true. The lawyer remains suspicious, however, because her vision
smacks of religious enthusiasm, and at the end of her testimony, he
predicts that she will be 'hanged yet' (439). Ayscough is also troubled
by the fact that Rebecca's vision is a rich and elaborate one, and one
that he would not have expected of an all-but-illiterate prostitute. In
other words, he is unwilling to grant that a member of the lower
orders could possibly have had the experience she claims to have had.
It is for that reason that Fowles includes Ayscough's conversation with

Wardley in the novel: he wants to emphasise that Rebecca's religious convictions, and those of her (as yet unborn) daughter Ann, are almost wholly independent of Wardley's. Indeed, he goes so far as to say of Ann's vision that it is

> more thoroughgoing than Wesley's, a fact that we may attribute in part to her sex, but perhaps above all to the fact that she was uneducated; that is, unsullied by stock belief, learned tradition, and the influence of the other kind of enlightenment. At heart people like Ann were revolutionaries; one with the very first Christians of all, and their founder. (457)

The 'influence of the other kind of enlightenment' is, of course, that of the Age of Reason, an age concerned more to preserve the status quo than to admit of change, and concerned, too, more with humanity in the mass than with the feelings of the individual. If Ann Lee was a revolutionary, it was in the sense that she rejected the teaching of the established church in favour of her own religious convictions, born of revelation. Yet she was a revolutionary before her time, dying in 1784, just before the French Revolution and the beginnings of the Romantic Movement.

And now we see, perhaps more clearly than before, why Rebecca's experience of spiritual nakedness echoes a passage in Book IV of Wordsworth's *The Prelude*. Fowles wants to claim Ann Lee and her fictional mother Rebecca as harbingers of the Romantic celebration of individual experience, for it was Wordsworth who claimed, in reaction against the Age of Reason, that poetry was 'the spontaneous overflow of powerful feelings' recollected in tranquillity. Many people, Ann Lee amongst them, brought an essentially Romantic sensibility to the England of the early eighteenth century, well in advance of the Romantic Movement, and are accordingly, Fowles suggests, worthy of both our attention and respect. But this is a purely personal view of history, one that is voiced not within an academic historical study, nor even within a historical novel, but instead, within a work that Fowles describes, idiosyncratically, as 'a maggot'.

Notes

1 Introduction

1. See Mark Amory, 'Tales Out of School', *Sunday Times Magazine* (22 September 1974) 34, where Fowles says, 'if there is one thing that all the books I like have it is narrative; and if there is an author whose star I am under it is Defoe.'

2. Another reason why Fowles is a best-selling author is that three of his novels – *The Collector*, *The Magus* and *The French Lieutenant's Woman* – and one of his short stories, 'The Ebony Tower', have been made into films. Though discussion of these films lies outside the scope of this study, I have included some articles and a book on the films of *The Collector*, *The Magus* and *The French Lieutenant's Woman* in the bibliography for those who wish to read about them.

3. John Fowles, quoted by Lorna Sage, in 'John Fowles: a Profile', *New Review*, 1 (7 October 1974) 35.

4. Sarah Benton, 'Adam and Eve', *New Socialist*, 11 (May–June 1983) 19.

5. Ibid.

6. John Fowles, *The Aristos* (1964, revised 1968; rev. version rpt. London: Triad Grafton, 1986) p. 157. All quotations are from this edition; page numbers will be given in the text.

7. See Benton, 19, for Fowles's comment that he is aware that *Mantissa* is not as good as his other fictions, and should not have been published.

8. Ibid.

9. Katherine Tarbox, *The Art of John Fowles* (Athens/London: University of Georgia Press, 1988) p. 188.

10. Jung sets out his theory of the anima (and animus, the male component to be found in women), in 'The Relations Between the Ego and the Unconscious', in *Two Essays on Analytical Psychology*, trans. R.F.C. Hull (London: Routledge & Kegan Paul, 1953). See Tarbox, p. 190, where Fowles comments that the Muse and the anima are one. For a

book-length discussion of Fowles's interest in Jung, see Carol Barnum, *The Fiction of John Fowles: a Myth for Our Time* (Greenwood, FL: Penkevill Publ. Co., 1988).

11. Mark Amory, 'Tales Out of School', *Sunday Times Magazine*, (22 September 1974) 33.
12. Ibid.
13. Ibid.
14. John Fowles, quoted by Roy Newquist, in 'John Fowles', *Counterpoint* (Chicago: Rand-McNally, 1964) pp. 218–19.
15. John Fowles, 'I Write Therefore I Am', *Evergreen Review*, 8 (August–September 1964) 17.
16. Ibid., p. 90.
17. John Fowles, quoted by James Campbell, in 'An Interview with John Fowles', *Contemporary Literature*, 17 (Autumn 1976) 465.
18. Newquist, p. 225.
19. Ibid., pp. 224–5.

2 *The Collector*

1. Quoted in John Baker, 'John Fowles', *Publishers Weekly* (25 November 1974) 6, and Richard Boston, 'John Fowles, Alone But Not Lonely', *New York Times Book Review* (9 November 1969) 2.
2. John Fowles, 'I Write Therefore I Am', *Evergreen Review*, 8 (August–September 1964) 89.
3. See Susana Onega, *Form and Meaning in the Novels of John Fowles* (Ann Arbor: UMI Research Press, 1989) pp. 188–9.
4. See Barry Olshen, *John Fowles* (New York: Ungar, 1978) p. 20.
5. Roy Newquist, 'John Fowles', in *Counterpoint* (Chicago: Rand-McNally) p. 225.
6. 'I Write Therefore I Am', *Evergreen Review*, 8 (August–September 1964) 17. See also James Baker, 'An Interview with John Fowles', *Michigan Quarterly Review*, 25 (Fall 1986) 667, where Fowles says, 'What I like about Defoe is his inventiveness, the way he can fake history so well, as he did in the *Journal of the Plague Year*. I like his narrative drive: he's a superb narrative novelist. ...It's a paradox, really: he wants to entertain people and to instruct them. I like that twin drive in him; which goes with this obviously very cunning mind behind the scenes, which so enjoys making things seem real.'
7. *The Aristos*, p. 9.
8. Daniel Defoe, *Moll Flanders*, ed. James Sutherland (Boston: Houghton Mifflin, 1959) p. 166. All quotations are from this edition.
9. Simon Loveday draws attention to Clegg's use of clichés and euphemisms in *The Romances of John Fowles* (London: Macmillan, 1985) p. 20, but reaches different conclusions from mine.
10. Newquist, p. 219.

3   *The Magus*

1. See John Fowles, 'Why I Rewrote *The Magus*', in *Saturday Review* (18 February 1978), rpt. in *Critical Essays on John Fowles*, ed. Ellen Pifer (Boston: G.K. Hall) p. 95.
2. Ibid., pp. 93–4.
3. See Fowles's foreword to *The Magus: a Revised Version* (London: Triad/Panther, 1977) p. 7. All quotations are from this edition, which Fowles clearly prefers; page numbers will be given in the text. An extended discussion of the differences between the two versions lies beyond the scope of this study. For a fuller account of Fowles's alterations, see the essay cited in note 1, as well as Ronald Binns' 'A New Version of *The Magus*', *Critical Quarterly*, 19 (Winter 1977) 79–84, and Michael Boccia's '"Visions and Revisions": John Fowles's New Version of *The Magus*', *Journal of Modern Literature*, 8 (1980–81) 234–6.
4. In 'John Fowles' *The Magus*: an Allegory of Self-Realization', *Journal of Popular Culture*, 9 (Spring 1976) 922, Barry Olshen notes that the seventy-eight chapters of the novel correspond to the seventy-eight cards in the Tarot deck, but finds 'little correlation between individual cards and chapters'.
5. See *The Magus*, p. 7, where Fowles reveals that Phraxos is based on the real Greek island of Spetsai, where he was employed as a teacher from 1951–52.
6. Quoted by James Campbell, in 'An Interview with John Fowles', *Contemporary Literature*, 17 (Autumn 1976) 466.
7. See p. 224, where Conchis says that he himself studied under Jung in the twenties. See also Carol Barnum, *The Fiction of John Fowles: a Myth for Our Time* (Greenwood, FL: Penkevill Publ. Co., 1988), for both an account of Fowles's interest in Jung and a Jungian reading of his fiction.
8. C.G. Jung, 'Commentary on "The Secret of the Golden Flower"' (1929), in *Alchemical Studies*, trans. R.F.C. Hull (London: Routledge & Kegan Paul, 1953) p. 52.
9. C.G. Jung, 'The Relations Between the Ego and the Unconscious', in *Two Essays in Analytical Psychology*, trans. R.F.C. Hull (London: Routledge & Kegan Paul, 1953) p. 236.
10. See Fowles's comment in the Foreword to the novel, that 'I did intend Conchis to exhibit a series of masks representing human notions of God, from the supernatural to the jargon-ridden scientific; that is, a series of human illusions about something that does not exist in fact, absolute knowledge and absolute power' (10). See also Fowles's 'My Recollections of Kafka', *Mosaic*, 3 (Summer 1970) 37, where he reveals that 'Two alternative titles to *The Magus* were *The Maze* and *The Godgame*...'

11. In 'The Fool's Journey: John Fowles's *The Magus*' (1966), in *Old Lines, New Forces: Essays on the Contemporary Novel, 1960–1970*, ed. Robert D. Morris (Rutherford: Fairleigh Dickinson U.P., 1976) p. 89, Marvin Magalener comments that the name 'de Seitas, perhaps associated with the medieval Latin *seitas* (oneself), may underline the importance of selfhood, the recognition of the reality of Self.' At this point in the novel, Urfe is developing a greater sense of self-knowledge: in existential terms, he is approaching a sense of authenticity, a sense that he must continue to develop for the rest of his life.

12. See *The French Lieutenant's Woman* (1969; rpt. London: Panther, 1972) pp. 13, 143, 163 and 224.

13. The phrase appears in the original version of *The Magus*, too (see John Fowles, *The Magus* [London: Jonathan Cape, 1966] p. 617). Cf. James Joyce, *A Portrait of the Artist as a Young Man* (1916; rpt. Harmondsworth, Middlesex: Penguin, 1973) p. 217, where Joyce says that 'in the virgin womb of [Stephen's] imagination the word was made flesh'. In his 'anagram made flesh', Fowles is partly acknowledging the obvious – that neither Urfe nor Alison are virgins – and is also hinting, more importantly, that, whether they marry or not, they will, as in Matthew 19.5, 'cleave' together and will 'be one flesh'.

4   *The French Lieutenant's Woman*

1. John Fowles, 'Notes on an Unfinished Novel', ed. Malcolm Bradbury, in *The Novel Today* (Manchester: Manchester University Press, 1977) p. 136.

2. 'Notes on an Unfinished Novel', p. 140.

3. Ibid., p. 139.

4. One of the best short definitions of existential authenticity is to be found in Mary Warnock's *Existentialism* (Oxford: Oxford University Press, 1979) p. 55: 'Authentic existence can only begin... once we have grasped... that each human being is, uniquely, himself and no one else, and that each of us has his own possibilities to fulfil[;] then our concern with the world, instead of being a mere concern to do as people in general do, ...can become *authentic* concern, to fulfil our real potentiality in the world.'

5. See John Fowles, 'Hardy and the Hag', in *Thomas Hardy After Fifty Years*, ed. Lance St John Butler (London: Macmillan, 1977) pp. 28–42. 1867 is also an important year for Hardy, as Fowles notes at the end of Chapter 35 of *The French Lieutenant's Woman*.

6. Cf. Jean-Paul Sartre's comment in 'M. François Mauriac et la liberté', in *Situations*, 1 (Paris 1947): 'You want your characters to live? Make them free' (my translation). Thomas Docherty draws attention to this passage

in 'A Constant Reality: the Presentation of Character in the Fiction of John Fowles', *Novel*, 14 (Winter 1981) 120.

7. That the characters are only *ostensibly* autonomous needs to be emphasised, for in 1976 Fowles said in an interview: 'It's silly to say the novelist isn't God, ...because... when you write a book you are... a tyrant, you are the total dictator.... [I]t's very difficult for a character in the book to stand up and say, you cannot do that, or I demand that that line be changed.' (Quoted by James Campbell in 'An Interview with John Fowles', *Contemporary Literature*, 17 [Autumn 1976] 463.)

8. In 'The French Lieutenant's Woman: Novel, Screenplay, Film', *Critical Quarterly*, 24 (Spring 1982) 45, Peter Conradi notes that James Antony Froude's *The Lieutenant's Daughter* (1847) and Dickens's *Great Expectations* (1860–1) are two of a number of Victorian novels that have alternative endings.

9. Charles Scruggs, 'The Two Endings of *The French Lieutenant's Woman*', *Modern Fiction Studies*, 31 (Spring 1985) 98.

10. See Fowles's self-conscious comment in Chapter 55: '...the conventions of Victorian fiction allow, allowed no place for the open, the inconclusive ending; and I preached earlier of the freedom characters must be given' (348).

11. In 'Fowles's *The French Lieutenant's Woman* as Tragedy', *Critique: Studies in Modern Fiction*, 13 (1972) 60, Prescott Evarts comments that Fowles 'immerses [his characters] in a plot that marches as simply as a classical tragedy'; however, he does not develop this point in detail. In '"The Unplumb'd, Salt Estranging" Tragedy of *The French Lieutenant's Woman*', *American Imago*, 42 (1985) 72, Douglas Johnstone says that the novel is 'a Shakespearean tragedy', but he uses the term 'tragedy' very loosely – for the most part, as a synonym for 'misfortune'.

12. *Aristotle's Poetics: a Translation and Commentary for Students of Literature*, trans. Leon Golden; commentary by O.B. Hardison, Jr (Englewood Cliffs, NJ: Prentice-Hall, 1968) p. 22.

13. Cf. Fowles's comment to Melvyn Bragg that 'practically everyone's assumed the central character is the heroine Sarah. But for me the book was always equally about Charles.' (Quoted in Bruce Woodcock, *Male Mythologies: John Fowles and Masculinity* [Brighton: Harvester, 1984] p. 85).

14. Fowles draws attention to Sarah's lance-like eyes again in *The French Lieutenant's Woman*, pp. 143, 163 and 224.

15. See *The French Lieutenant's Woman*, p. 16, for Fowles's comments on Marx.

16. As is clear from *The French Lieutenant's Woman*, pp. 64–5, Charles's feelings are at once sexual, fraternal and paternal.

17. Sarah is compared with the Sphinx in *The French Lieutenant's Woman*, pp. 376 and 399.

18. Cf. *David Copperfield*, Chapter 47, where the prostitute Martha seeks to drown herself in the Thames.

19. In '*The French Lieutenant's Woman*: the Unconscious Significance of a Novel to its Author', *American Imago*, 29 (1972) 169, Gilbert Rose argues that Charles 'has reconstituted [his mother] in both idealised and devalued forms' in Sarah Woodruff and the prostitute Sarah. Each Sarah's daughter, says Rose, 'is his stillborn sister...' Fowles finds this interpretation attractive in 'Hardy and the Hag', p. 31.

20. Scruggs, 99. Scruggs is referring here, of course, to the main character of Samuel Richardson's novel *Pamela* (1740).

21. In 'John Fowles: a Novelist's Dilemma', *Saturday Review* (October 1981) 40, Joshua Gilder quotes Fowles as saying: 'I deliberately did not tell anyone what was going on in [Sarah's] mind'.

22. Cf. Mary Warnock, *Existentialism* (London: Oxford University Press, 1970) pp. 57–98.

23. In 'Cryptic Coloration in *The French Lieutenant's Woman*', *Journal of Narrative Technique*, 3 (1973) 204, and *The Romances of John Fowles* (London: Macmillan, 1985) p. 59, Elizabeth Rankin and Simon Loveday, respectively, present a similar view of the novel's second ending. Scruggs, p. 102, identifies the melodramatic element: 'When [Sarah] accepts Charles in [Chapter 60], it would be easy to define her within the context of a Victorian cliché or a combination of several Victorian clichés: Fallen Woman redeemed by True Love or Woman finds True Self in Marriage.'

24. It may be that Fowles has Sydney Carton, of Dickens's *A Tale of Two Cities*, in mind here: Carton nobly goes to the guillotine in place of another character, Charles Darnay.

5　*The Ebony Tower*

1. Simon Loveday, *The Romances of John Fowles* (London: Macmillan, 1985) p. 82; Mel Gussow, 'Talk with John Fowles', *New York Times Book Review* (13 November 1977) 84.

2. Quoted in John Baker, 'John Fowles', *Publishers Weekly* (25 November 1974) 7. However, Fowles has also said that in writing the title story of the collection, 'I wanted to de-mystify *The Magus*, which I think was altogether too full of mystery. ["The Ebony Tower"] is a kind of realistic version of *The Magus*.' (Quoted by Robert Robinson, in 'Giving the Reader a Choice: a Conversation with John Fowles', *The Listener* [31 October 1974] 584.)

3. Baker, 7. Similarly, Robinson, 584, quotes Fowles as having said that he 'certainly didn't think, "I'll do a variation on some past story"...'

4. John Fowles, quoted by Christopher Bigsby, in *The Radical Imagination and the Liberal Tradition*, ed. Heide Ziegler and Christopher Bigsby (London: Junction Books, 1982) p. 117.
5. John Fowles, quoted by Susana Onega, in *Form and Meaning in the Novels of John Fowles* (Ann Arbor: UMI Research Press, 1989) p. 181.
6. John Fowles, quoted by Katherine Tarbox, in *The Art of John Fowles* (Athens: University of Georgia Press, 1988) p. 186.
7. See note 4.
8. Quoted in Joshua Gilder, 'John Fowles: a Novelist's Dilemma', *Saturday Review* (October 1981) 39. See also John Fowles, 'Downandoutdom', [Review of *Four Novellas*, by Samuel Beckett (London: John Calder, 1978)], *Irish Press*, 16 February 1978, The Book Page, where Fowles speaks of 'the ebony tower of total self-involvement'.
9. Roy Newquist, 'John Fowles', in *Counterpoint* (Chicago: Rand McNally, 1964) pp. 224–5.
10. In 'Fictional Self-Consciousness in John Fowles's *The Ebony Tower*', *Ariel*, 16 (July 1985) 21–38, Frederick M. Holmes argues, similarly, that in *The Ebony Tower*, the 'resources of fiction [are shown to] no longer lend themselves to the discovery of important truths about life' (21).
11. See Lewis Carroll, *The Annotated Alice*, ed. Martin Gardner (Harmondsworth: Penguin, 1970) p. 95. Carroll leaves the riddle unanswered; though various answers to it have been suggested (see p. 95, n3), no single answer can be said to be the definitive one.
12. Robert Robinson, 'Giving the Reader a Choice: a Conversation with John Fowles', 584.
13. Roland Barthes, *Mythologies*, trans. Annette Lavers (1957; London: Paladin, 1973) pp. 81–4.
14. *Hamlet*. IV.v.181.
15. Quoted in Carol M. Barnum, *The Fiction of John Fowles: a Myth for Our Time* (Greenwood, FL: Penkevill Publ. Co., 1988) p. 99, n11.
16. Ibid., n12.
17. John Fowles, quoted in *The Radical Imagination and the Liberal Tradition*, ed. Heide Ziegler and Christopher Bigsby (London: Junction Books, 1982) p. 117.

6 Daniel Martin

1. John Fowles, quoted by Susana Onega, in *Form and Meaning in the Novels of John Fowles* (Ann Arbor: UMI Research Press, 1989) p. 178.
2. In 'Talk with John Fowles', *New York Times Book Review* (13 November 1977) 84, Mel Gussow notes that '[b]oth the revised *Magus* and... *The Ebony Tower* were written during the creation of *Daniel Martin*.'

3. Matthew Arnold, 'To a Friend' (1849), in *Victorian Poetry and Poetics*, ed. Walter E. Houghton and G. Robert Stange (Boston: Houghton Mifflin, 1959) p. 395.

4. Cf. Fowles's essay, 'Seeing Nature Whole', *Harper's Magazine*, 259 (November 1979) 49–68, and in particular the passage where he says, 'What is irreplaceable in any object of art is never, in the final analysis, its technique or craft, but the personality of the artist, the expression of his unique and individual feeling' (55). If we were to substitute 'being' for 'feeling' here, 'his unique and individual being' would be a good synonym for 'authenticity' – for what the artist (or indeed, any individual) 'sees' with 'whole sight'.

5. 'He had not', Fowles says of Charles in *The French Lieutenant's Woman*, 'the benefit of existentialist terminology; but what he felt was really a very clear case of the anxiety of freedom – that is, the realisation that one is free and the realisation that being free is a situation of terror' (296). For Fowles's comment on Jane Austen, quoted in the last chapter, see Roy Newquist, 'John Fowles', in *Counterpoint* (Chicago: Rand McNally, 1964) pp. 224–5.

6. Onega, p. 181.

7. See Fowles's comment to James Baker that 'Dan is a little bit myself, but [with respect to writing plays], absolutely not. And I'm a lousy filmscript writer, never had any talent for it.' ('An Interview with John Fowles', *Michigan Quarterly Review*, 25 [Fall 1986] 672.) See also Gussow, 84, where Fowles comments that 'I was brought up in a Devon village, the one in the book. Quite a lot of my ideas are spoken by [Dan]. I gave him two or three of my interests in common[:] each [of us] is an amateur botanist, with a passion for orchids. Martin covets idyllic places (such as Bandelier National Monument in New Mexico) calling each *la bonne vaux*, "the valley of abundance, the sacred combe".' Fowles, Gussow adds, 'shares this love of landscape'.

8. John Fowles, quoted by James Baker, 'An Interview with John Fowles', 665–6.

9. See Charles Dickens, *David Copperfield* (1849–50; rpt. Harmondsworth: Middlesex, 1970) p. 11. See also Robert Foulke, 'A Conversation with John Fowles', *Salmagundi*, 68–9 (Fall 1985–Winter 1986) 380, where Fowles says, 'I'm convinced I've found a valuable way of reliving the past which is imaginatively right... In *Daniel Martin*... it's clear that anyone might consider some childhood [experience] closer to him than an event that happened yesterday.'

10. Why he says this is rather puzzling, for flashbacks and flashes forward in time are a staple of modern cinematography. What he seems to mean is that film can only *record* the present, while it must fictionalise the past or future.

11. Matthew Arnold, 'Stanzas from the Grande Chartreuse', in *Victorian Poetry and Poetics*, ed. Walter E. Houghton and G. Robert Stange (Boston: Houghton Mifflin, 1959) p. 463, ll. 85–6.

12. See *Daniel Martin*, p. 170: 'The 1951 Festival of Britain was not at all the herald of a new age, but the death-knell of the old one [in context, the world of Victorian-influenced Britain]. See also Baker, 674, where Fowles says that 'Behind most of my books I have some great model[,]... and the one behind *Daniel Martin* was definitely Flaubert's *Sentimental Education.*' From this comment, and another like it in an interview with Carol Barnum, it is clear that, just as Flaubert described the attitudes and opinions of a nineteenth-century French generation in *A Sentimental Education*, so Fowles sought to present those of his own generation – and, in particular, of his own social class – in *Daniel Martin*. (See Carol Barnum, 'An Interview with John Fowles', *Modern Fiction Studies*, 31 [Spring 1985] 200.)

13. Fowles's views on the distinction between being British and being English, as relayed to us by Dan, clearly derive from 'On Being English but Not British', an essay Fowles published in *Texas Quarterly*, 7 (Autumn 1964) 154–62, and also from 'Seeing Nature Whole', cited above, n4).

14. Cf. Fowles's comment to Christopher Bigsby in 1982, quoted in the last chapter: 'I now think of existentialism as a kind of literary metaphor, a wish fulfilment. I long ago began to doubt whether it had any true philosophical value in many of its assertions about freedom.' *The Radical Imagination and the Liberal Tradition*, ed. Heide Ziegler and Christopher Bigsby (London: Junction Books, 1982) p. 117.

15. See Fowles's comment to Raman Singh, that *Daniel Martin* is 'basically about the English, Englishness; what are the English?... And it [is] also about my generation, my middle-class Oxford generation of the English which, I think, is generally a sad and failed one.' ('An Encounter with John Fowles', *Journal of Modern Literature*, 8 [1980/81] 187.)

16. This passage is less surprising if read in conjunction with 'Seeing Nature Whole', where Fowles argues more fully that what it is to be English is a function of the Englishman's origins as a forest dweller, and comments at greater length on the Englishness of Robin Hood.

17. Sue Park says much the same thing about this scene in her excellent 'Time and Ruins in John Fowles's *Daniel Martin*', *Modern Fiction Studies*, 31 (Spring 1985) 157–63.

7 *A Maggot*

1. John Fowles, quoted in *The Radical Imagination and the Liberal Tradition*, ed. Heide Ziegler and Christopher Bigsby (London: Junction Books, 1982) p. 123.

2. In James Baker's 'An Interview with John Fowles', *Michigan Quarterly Review*, 25 (Fall 1986) 661–83, Fowles says that he insisted on the title, despite his publisher's objections, because 'I am not interested in becoming just a best-selling author who always picks suitable titles...' (662).

3. Baker, 671.

4. That *A Maggot* is an extended variation on 'The Enigma' has been said so often that it is now a critical commonplace.

5. Fowles not only read but edited John Aubrey's *Monumenta Britannica, or a Miscellany of British Antiquities*, annotated by Rodney Legg (Boston: Little, Brown, 1980). As Fowles points out in the preface, *Monumenta Britannica* was completed in the late seventeenth century, but remained unpublished until Legg's edition made its appearance in 1980. Fowles refers to Pastor Moritz's *Travels in England in 1782* in an interview with Christopher Bigsby, in *The Radical Imagination and the Liberal Tradition*, p. 115, and again in his prefatory essay to Fay Godwin's *Land* (London: Heinemann, 1985) p. xiii. While he does not specify which edition he read, it would most probably have been the 1795 translation of *Travels of Carl Philipp Moritz in England in 1782*, intro. P.E. Matheson (1795; rpt. London: Humphrey Milford, 1924), from which all quotations are taken.

6. See Baker, 664, and Robert Foulke, 'A Conversation with John Fowles', *Salmagundi*, 68–9 (Fall 1985–Winter 1986), 370–1, 379.

7. Foulke, 370–1. See also Baker, 663, where Fowles says, 'I had a lot of fun trying to imitate the language [of the period], but... if you put my language into a university department for assessment people would knock holes through it.'

8. Baker, 668. See also Baker, 663, where Fowles says, 'The purpose of some novels is to give a personal summary of how *you* yourself see history. This is not what the true historian is usually trying to do.'

9. Foulke, 367.

10. Ibid., 368.

11. Ibid.

12. Baker, 668.

13. Similarly, in Chapter 61 of *The French Lieutenant's Woman*, Fowles's third-person narrator observes Charles and Sarah from the street outside the house in which they meet for the last time.

14. Pierre Monnin, 'Cumulative Strangeness Without and Within *A Maggot* by J. Fowles', in *On Strangeness*, ed. Margaret Bridges (Tübingen: Narr,

1990, Swiss Papers on English Language and Literature, vol. 5) pp. 151, 153.

15. The similarities between the towns are compelling. C– has 'a few hundred inhabitants' (14), and is dominated by a high-pinnacled church, while Castleton is 'a small town' (*Travels of Carl Philipp Moritz in England in 1782*, p. 184), over which an ancient castle towers. Near C– is the cavern in which Rebecca experiences June Eternal; to reach it, the travellers must cross a stream. To reach the cavern near Castleton, a stream must also be crossed: the man who carries Pastor Moritz over it 'struck me as a real Charon' (*Travels*, p. 185), while Rebecca says that the cavern she visited looked at first 'like a gateway to Hell' (358). Inside the Castleton cavern, Moritz sees 'the Majesty of the Creator displayed' in a 'subterranean Temple, in the structure of which no human hand had borne a part' (*Travels*, pp. 190–1), while in her cavern Rebecca experiences June Eternal, another sign of the Creator's glory.

16. John Fowles, quoted by Katherine Tarbox, in *The Art of John Fowles* (Athens: University of Georgia Press, 1988) p. 186.

17. Ibid., p. 139.

18. See George Sarton, *A History of Science: Ancient Science Through the Golden Age of Greece* (London: Oxford University Press, 1953) p. 214ff. Pythagoras and his followers attached special significance to a number of ratios, including those of the vibration numbers on a stringed instrument: 12:6, 12:8 and 8:6. 'The numbers 12, 8 [and] 6 form a harmonic proportion. …The idea of harmonic proportion was soon extended to astronomy. The heavenly spheres were supposed to be separated by musical intervals and the planets emitted different notes in harmony' (214). It is also significant that his Lordship's former mathematics tutor at Cambridge, Saunderson, dismisses the young man's theories as 'phantasies rather than probable or experimental truths' (194). They are the theories not of a mathematician, he implies, but of a misguided dreamer. It is also significant that his Lordship anticipates Wordsworth in believing that God is immanent in nature – an idea to which Wordsworth gives expression in 'Tintern Abbey' and *The Prelude*. (Here I am grateful to my colleague Gordon Spence, a Romantic poetry specialist, for pointing out to me that there are many eighteenth-century poets who anticipate Wordsworth in believing that God is immanent in nature – one of the best examples being James Thomson, author of *The Seasons* [1730]).

19. In John Fowles and Barry Brukoff, *The Enigma of Stonehenge* (London: Jonathan Cape, 1980) pp. 93–105, Fowles points out that John Aubrey originally suggested, very tentatively, that the Druids may have built Stonehenge. The idea was subsequently taken up by William Stukeley, who 'ignoring all Aubrey's qualifications… became "blindly certain" (105) that the Druids had constructed it'.

20. *The Concise Oxford Dictionary of Current English*, ed. R.E. Allen (Oxford: Clarendon Press, 1990) p. 743.
21. *The Enigma of Stonehenge*, p. 74.
22. It may be that in 'You are she I have sought'(328), Fowles is echoing Robert Burns's 'The Cotter's Saturday Night' (1786), where the cotter enjoins his children to 'Implore His counsel and assisting might:/ They never sought in vain that sought the Lord aright!'
23. Luke 23.34
24. See Baker, 672, where Fowles says that 'June Eternal was meant to be a foreshadowing of the living Shaker communities... What I was really trying to suggest was that in these weird visions... a lot of these very uncultivated dissenters were seeing considerable truths, or hopes, for mankind; and I thought to illustrate the difference between the often very primitive conditions or actual details of these visions and the great truths lying behind them.'
25. William Wordsworth, *The Prelude: a Parallel Text*, ed. J.C. Maxwell (1805, 1850; rpt. Harmondsworth: Penguin, 1970) p. 146. (I have quoted from the 1805 text here.)
26. Cf. William Blake's, 'If the doors of perception were cleansed, every thing would appear to man as it is, infinite. For man has closed himself up, till he sees all things thro' narrow chinks of his cavern.' ('The Marriage of Heaven and Hell', in *Romantic Poetry and Prose*, ed. Russell Noyes [New York: Oxford University Press, 1956] p. 213.)
27. See Carol Barnum, *The Fiction of John Fowles: a Myth for Our Time* (Greenwood, FL: Penkevill, 1988) pp. 128–44, and Susana Onega, *Form and Meaning in the Novels of John Fowles* (Ann Arbor: UMI Research Press, 1989), pp. 137–63.

Select Bibliography

WORKS BY JOHN FOWLES

Novels and Short Stories

The dates of the first editions of Fowles's short stories and novels are given below, followed by the dates and other bibliographical details of the reprinted editions cited in the foregoing chapters.

The Collector. London: Cape; Boston: Little Brown, 1963. Rpt. London: Triad/Panther, 1976.

The Magus. Boston: Little Brown, 1965; London: Cape, 1966. Revised version, Cape, 1977; Boston: Little Brown, 1978. Revised version rpt. London: Triad/Panther, 1978.

The French Lieutenant's Woman. London: Cape; Boston: Little Brown, 1969. Rpt. London: Panther, 1972.

The Ebony Tower. London: Cape; Boston: Little Brown, 1974. Rpt. London: Pan, 1986.

Daniel Martin. London: Cape; Boston: Little Brown, 1977. Rpt. London: Triad/Grafton, 1986.

Mantissa. London: Cape; Boston: Little Brown, 1982. Rpt. London: Triad/Grafton, 1986.

A Maggot. London: Cape; Boston: Little Brown, 1985. Rpt. London: Pan, 1986.

Selected essays and interviews

Amory, Mark 'Tales Out of School', *Sunday Times Magazine*, (22 September 1974) 33–5.

Baker, James R. 'An Interview with John Fowles'. *Michigan Quarterly Review*, 25 (Fall 1986) 661–83.

Baker, John 'John Fowles'. *Publishers' Weekly*, (25 Nov. 1974) 6–7.

Barnum, Carol 'An Interview with John Fowles'. *Contemporary Literature*, 17 (1976), 455–69.

Benton, Sarah 'Adam and Eve'. *New Socialist*, 11 (May–June 1983) 18–19.

Bigsby, C.W.E. 'John Fowles'. In *The Radical Imagination and the Liberal Tradition*. Ed. Heide Ziegler and C.W.E. Bigsby. London: Junction Books, 1982, pp. 111–25.

Boston, Richard 'John Fowles, Alone But Not Lonely'. *New York Times Book Review* (9 November 1969) 2, 52–3.

Campbell, James 'An Interview with John Fowles'. *Contemporary Literature*, 17 (Autumn 1976) 455–69.

Foulke, Robert 'A Conversation with John Fowles'. *Salmagundi*, 68–9 (Fall 1985–Winter 1986) 367–84.

Fowles, John 'I Write Therefore I Am'. *Evergreen Review*, 8 (August–September 1964) 16–17, 89–90.

Fowles, John 'On Being English But Not British'. *Texas Quarterly*, 7 (Autumn 1964) 154–62.

Fowles, John 'My Recollections of Kafka'. *Mosaic*, 3 (Summer 1970) 31–41.

Fowles, John 'Notes on an Unfinished Novel'. In *The Novel Today*. Ed. Malcolm Bradbury. Manchester: Manchester University Press, 1977, pp. 136–50.

Fowles, John 'Hardy and the Hag'. In *Thomas Hardy After Fifty Years*. Ed. Lance St John Butler. London: Macmillan, 1977, pp. 28–42.

Fowles, John 'Why I Rewrote *The Magus*'. In *Saturday Review* (18 February 1978) 25–7, 30. Rpt. in *Critical Essays on John Fowles*. Ed. Ellen Pifer. (Boston: G.K. Hall, 1986), pp. 93–9.

Fowles, John 'Seeing Nature Whole'. *Harper's Magazine*, 259 (November 1979) 49–68.

Gussow, Mel 'Talk with John Fowles'. *New York Times Book Review* (13 November 1977) 3, 84–5.

Halpern, Daniel 'A Sort of Exile in Lyme Regis'. *London Magazine*, NS 10, 12 (1971) 34–46.

Newquist, Roy 'John Fowles'. *Counterpoint* (Chicago: Rand-McNally, 1964) pp. 218–25.

Onega, Susana 'Fowles on Fowles'. In *Form and Meaning in the Novels of John Fowles*. Ann Arbor: UMI Research Press, 1989.

Robinson, Robert 'Giving the Reader a Choice: a Conversation with John Fowles'. *The Listener*, 31 October 1974, 584.

Sage, Lorna 'John Fowles: a Profile'. *New Review*, 1, 7 (1974) 31–7.

Singh, Raman 'An Encounter with John Fowles'. *Journal of Modern Literature*, 8 (1980–81) 181–202.

Selected criticism

Baker, James R. and Diane Vipond eds. *Twentieth Century Literature*, 42 (Spring 1996). Special Fowles Issue.

Barnum, Carol *The Fiction of John Fowles: a Myth for Our Time*. Greenwood, FL: Penkevill Publ. Co., 1988.

Binns, Ronald 'A New Version of *The Magus*'. *Critical Quarterly*, 19 (Winter 1977) 79–84.

Boccia, Michael '"Visions and Revisions": John Fowles's New Version of *The Magus*'. *Journal of Modern Literature*, 8 (1980–81) 235–46.

Butler, Lance St John 'John Fowles and the Fiction of Freedom'. In *The British and Irish Novel Since 1960*. Ed. James Acheson. London: Macmillan/New York: St Martin's Press, 1991.

Conradi, Peter '*The French Lieutenant's Woman*: Novel, Screenplay, Film'. *Critical Quarterly*, 24 (Spring 1982) 41–57.

Corbett, Thomas 'The Film and the Book: a Case Study of *The Collector*'. *English Journal*, 57 (March 1968) 328–33.

Docherty, Thomas 'A Constant Reality: the Presentation of Character in the Fiction of John Fowles'. *Novel*, 14 (Winter 1981) 118–34.

Evarts, Prescott 'Fowles's *The French Lieutenant's Woman* as Tragedy'. *Critique: Studies in Modern Fiction*, 13, 3 (1972) 57–69.

Franklyn, A. Frederic 'The Hand in the Fist' [a study of William Wyler's film version of *The Collector*]. *Trace* (Spring 1966) 22–7, 101–7.

Garard, Charles *Point of View in Fiction and Film: Focus on John Fowles*. New York: Peter Lang, 1991.

Gilder, Joshua 'John Fowles: a Novelist's Dilemma', *Saturday Review* (October 1981) 36–40.

Holmes, Frederick 'Fictional Self-Consciousness in John Fowles's *The Ebony Tower*'. *Ariel*, 16 (July 1985) 21–38.

Johnstone, Douglas '"The Unplumb'd, Salt Estranging" Tragedy of *The French Lieutenant's Woman*'. *American Imago*, 42 (1985) 69–83.

Knapp, Shoshana 'The Transformation of a Pinter Screenplay: Freedom and Calculators in *The French Lieutenant's Woman*'. *Modern Drama*, 28 (March 1985) 55–70.

Lorsch, Susan 'Pinter Fails Fowles: Narration in *The French Lieutenant's Woman*'. *Literature/Film Quarterly*, 16 (1988) 144–54.

Loveday, Simon *The Romances of John Fowles*. London: Macmillan, 1985.

Magalener, Marvin 'The Fool's Journey: John Fowles's *The Magus* (1966). In *Old Lines, New Forces: Essays on the Contemporary Novel, 1960–1970*. Ed. Robert D. Martin. Rutherford: Fairleigh Dickinson University Press, 1976, pp. 81–92.

Olshen, Barry 'John Fowles's *The Magus*: an Allegory of Self-Realization'. *Journal of Popular Culture*, 9 (Spring 1976) 916–25.

Olshen, Barry *John Fowles*. New York: Ungar, 1978.

Palmer, William 'Fowles's *The Magus*: the Vortex as Myth, Metaphor, and Masque'. In *The Power of Myth in Literature and Film*. Ed. Victor Carrabino. Tallahassee: University of Florida Press, 1980, pp. 66–76.

Park, Sue 'Time and Ruins in John Fowles's *Daniel Martin*'. *Modern Fiction Studies*, 31 (Spring 1985) 157–63.

Rankin, Elizabeth 'Cryptic Coloration in *The French Lieutenant's Woman*'. *Journal of Narrative Technique*, 3 (1973) 193–207.

Rose, Gilbert '*The French Lieutenant's Woman*: the Unconscious Significance of a Novel to its Author'. *American Imago*, 29 (1972) 165–79.

Scruggs, Charles 'The Two Endings of *The French Lieutenant's Woman*'. *Modern Fiction Studies*, 31 (Spring 1985) 95–114.

Tarbox, Katherine *The Art of John Fowles*. Athens: University of Georgia Press, 1988.

Woodcock, Bruce *Male Mythologies: John Fowles and Masculinity*. Brighton: Harvester, 1984.

Index